THE ROVER BOYS AT COLBY HALL

OR, THE STRUGGLES OF THE YOUNG CADETS

ARTHUR M. WINFIELD

(Edward Stratemeyer)

1st WORLD
LIBRARY
Literary Society

The Rover Boys at Colby Hall

Arthur M. Winfield

© 1st World Library, 2007
PO Box 2211
Fairfield, IA 52556
www.1stworldlibrary.com
First Edition

LCCN: 2007934107

Softcover ISBN: 978-1-4218-9615-1
Hardcover ISBN: 978-1-4218-9715-8
eBook ISBN: 978-1-4218-9515-4

Purchase *"The Rover Boys at Colby Hall"*
as a traditional bound book at:
www.1stWorldLibrary.com/purchase.asp?ISBN=978-1-4218-9615-1

1st World Library is a literary, educational organization
dedicated to:

- Creating a free internet library of downloadable ebooks

- Hosting writing competitions and offering book publishing
scholarships.

1st World Library Literary Society

Giving Back to the World

"If you want to work on the core problem, it's early school literacy."

- James Barksdale, former CEO of Netscape

"No skill is more crucial to the future of a child, or to a democratic and prosperous society, than literacy."

- Los Angeles Times

"Literacy... means far more than learning how to read and write... The aim is to transmit... knowledge and promote social participation."

- UNESCO

"Literacy is not a luxury, it is a right and a responsibility. If our world is to meet the challenges of the twenty-first century we must harness the energy and creativity of all our citizens."

- President Bill Clinton

"Parents should be encouraged to read to their children, and teachers should be equipped with all available techniques for teaching literacy, so the varying needs and capacities of individual kids can be taken into account."

- Hugh Mackay

CONTENTS

INTRODUCTION

MY DEAR BOYS: This book is a complete story in itself, but forms the first volume in a line issued under the general title, "The Second Rover Boys Series for Young Americans."

As mentioned in several of the other volumes of the first series, this line was started a number of years ago with the publication of "The Rover Boys at School," in which my readers were introduced to Dick, Tom, and Sam Rover, three wide-awake American lads. In that volume and in those which followed I gave the particulars of their adventures while attending Putnam Hall Military Academy, Brill College, and while on numerous outings, both in our own country and abroad.

The Rover boys were, of course, growing older; and, having met three young ladies very much to their liking, each married and settled down, as related in detail in the several volumes immediately preceding this. They were well established in business; and in due course of time Dick Rover was blessed with a son, as was also Sam, while the fun-loving Tom became the proud possessor of a pair of twins who were as full of life as their father had ever been.

In this volume the younger Rover boys are old enough to go to boarding school. They are sent to Colby Hall Military

Academy, presided over by an old friend and schoolmate of their fathers; and there they make both friends and enemies, and have numerous adventures.

In the beginning this chronicle of the younger Rovers, I wish to thank my numerous readers for all the kind things they have said about the other volumes in these series, and I trust that they will make just as good friends of Jack, Andy and Randy, and Fred as they did of Dick, Tom, and Sam Rover.

Affectionately and sincerely yours,

EDWARD STRATEMEYER.

CHAPTER I

INTRODUCING THE YOUNGER ROVERS

"For gracious sake! what's that racket?" exclaimed Dick Rover, as he threw down the newspaper he was reading and leaped to his feet.

"Sounds to me as if there was a battle royal going on," returned his younger brother, Sam, who was at a desk in the library of the old farmhouse, writing a letter.

"It's those boys!" exclaimed Tom Rover, as he tossed aside a copy of a comic paper which he had been looking over. "I'll wager they're up to some mischief again."

"Well, if they are your boys, Tom, you mustn't find fault with them," answered Sam Rover, with a twinkle in his eye. "If ever there were chips of the old block, your twins are It with a capital I."

"Humph!" snorted Tom Rover. "I don't think Andy and Randy are much ahead of your Fred when it comes to playing tricks, and I think Dick's Jack can hold up his end too."

"Never mind about that just now," broke in Dick Rover,

hastily. "Let's go out and see what those kids are up to."

"All right. But don't be too severe with 'em," pleaded Tom Rover. "Remember, boys will be boys."

"That's true, Tom. But we've got to take 'em in hand sooner or later," remonstrated his brother Sam. "If we don't, they'll grow up the wildest bunch ever known."

A number of cries of alarm and protest, mingled with fierce cheering, had reached the house from the garden just beyond the broad veranda. As the three Rover brothers hurried through the hallway and outside, the yelling and cheering were renewed. Then, just as Tom Rover stepped out on the veranda, there was a sudden swish and a stream of water from a garden hose caught him directly in the left ear.

"Hi! Hi! Stop that!" cried Tom Rover, doing his best to dodge the stream of water, which suddenly seemed to play all over the piazza. "What do you mean by wetting me this way?"

"It wasn't my fault, Dad," came from a boy standing on the lawn, both hands clutching a rubber hose held, also, by another boy of about the same age. "It was Fred who turned the hose that way."

"Nothing of the sort! It was Randy twisted it that way trying to get it away from me," cried Fred Rover. "And he isn't going to do it!" and thereupon ensued a struggle between the two boys which caused the stream of water to fly over the garden first in one direction and then another.

In the meanwhile, not far away another stream of water was issuing from a hose held by two other lads. This, as well as the water from hose number one, had been directed towards the

Arthur M. Winfield

back of the garden, where an elderly white man and an equally elderly colored man were trying to shelter themselves behind a low hedge to keep from becoming drenched.

"Fo' de lan's' sake, Massa Dick! won't you make dem boys stop?" cried out the old colored man, when he caught sight of Dick Rover hurrying out on the lawn. "Dem boys is jest nacherly tryin' to drown old Aleck Pop, dat's what dey is!"

"They didn't have no call to touch them hoses," came from the elderly white man. "I tol' 'em they mustn't muss with the water; but they won't mind nohow!" and thus speaking old Jack Ness held up his hands in comic despair.

"Why! we didn't know you were behind the hedge," came from one of the boys holding the second hose. "We thought you were both down at the barn."

"You can't make believe like that, Andy Rover!" returned the old man of all work, shaking his head vigorously. "You knowed I was goin' to trim up this hedge a bit and that Aleck was goin' to help me."

"You boys let up with this nonsense," came sternly from Tom Rover. He turned to face one of his twins. "Randy, I ought to give you a thrashing for wetting me like this."

"Don't Fred get half the thrashing?" questioned Randy Rover, quizzically, for he could readily see that his parent was not as angry as his words seemed to imply. "I don't like to be selfish, you know. He can have more than his share if he wants it."

"You'll take your own thrashings—I don't want 'em," broke in his cousin Fred quickly.

"Jack," cried Dick Rover, turning to his son, "turn that water off at once."

"I don't know where to turn it off. I didn't turn it on," answered Jack Rover, the oldest of the four boys who had been fooling.

"I'll turn it off and fix it so they can't turn it on ag'in," came from old Jack Ness, and away hobbled the man of all work.

"I think it's a shame for you boys to drench old Ness and Aleck," was Sam Rover's sober comment. "Both of them might catch cold or get rheumatism."

"We didn't start to do anything like that, Dad," answered Fred Rover. "We were going to have a little fight between ourselves, playing rival firemen. We aimed the water at the hedge, and we didn't see Ness and Aleck until they let out a yell."

"But I saw two of you playing the water in that direction," cried Dick Rover. "You were one of them, Jack."

"Oh, well, Dad, what was the harm after they were all wet?" pleaded his son. "They'd have to change their clothing anyway."

"That's just it," added Andy Rover quickly, with his eyes twinkling from merriment. "A little more water won't hurt a person when he's already soaked. It's just like spoiling a rotten egg—it can't be done," and at this reply, both Dick Rover and his brother, the fun-loving Tom, had to turn away their faces to hide their amusement. Nevertheless, Dick sobered his face almost instantly as he answered:

"Well, these pranks around the farm have got to stop. You'll

Arthur M. Winfield

have your grandfather and Uncle Randolph and Aunt Martha all upset, not to say anything about your sisters and your mothers. It's a fortunate thing that they went down to the town to do some shopping. Otherwise I think all of you would be in for quite some punishment."

"Oh! Then you're not going to punish us, are you?" broke in Randy Rover quickly. "That's fine! I knew you wouldn't mind our having a little fun."

"Don't be so fast, young man," returned his father. "Your Uncle Dick may be too lenient. I am rather of the opinion that you and your brother, if not your cousins, have got to be taken in hand."

"Oh, please, Massa Tom, don' go fo' to punish 'em," burst out old Aleck Pop. "I—I don't s'pose dey meant any great ha'm, even do dey did t'row dat stream of wattah right in dis yere coon's mouf;" and he smiled broadly, showing a row of ivories, rather the worse for wear.

"I think all of you boys had better go into the house and get some dry clothing on before your mothers put in an appearance," suggested Dick Rover. "If they see you like this, all dripping wet, they'll certainly be worried."

"All right, Dad; I'll do it," answered Jack, quickly. And then he motioned to his cousins. "Come on, let's see how fast we can make the change;" and off into the big farmhouse rushed the boys, clattering up the back stairs one after the other, to the two big rooms which they occupied.

"Some boys!" was Sam Rover's comment, as he shook his head doubtfully.

"They are certainly growing older—and wilder," returned

Dick Rover.

"We've got to take them in hand—that is dead certain!" said Tom Rover, with conviction. "Why! if I don't do something with Andy and Randy pretty soon, they'll be as—as—"

"As bad as you were, Tom, at their age," finished Dick Rover, with a smile.

"Now you've said something, Dick," affirmed Sam Rover. "Andy isn't quite so bad when it comes to playing tricks, although he certainly says some awfully funny things, but when it comes to doing things Randy continually puts me in mind of Tom."

"Oh, say! To hear you fellows talk, you'd think that I was the worst boy that ever lived," grumbled Tom Rover. "What did I ever do to raise such a rumpus as this?"

"Phew! What did he ever do to raise such a rumpus as this?" mocked Sam Rover. "Well, what didn't he do? When father went to Africa and disappeared and we came down here to good old Valley Brook Farm, wasn't he the constant torment of Uncle Randolph and Aunt Martha, and the hired girl, and all the rest of the community until, in sheer despair, uncle had to send us off to Putnam Hall? And when we went to the Hall, who was the first one to get into trouble—exploding a giant firecracker on the campus? Answer me that, will you?"

"Ancient history," murmured Tom Rover, dryly. But then, of a sudden his eyes began to twinkle. "No use talking, though, we certainly did have some good times in those days, didn't we?" he continued. "Do you remember how we got the best of old Josiah Crabtree?"

"Yes. And how we got the best of a whole lot of our enemies,"

16   Arthur M. Winfield

added Sam Rover.

"Yes, and what gloriously good times we did have at Putnam Hall and at Brill College," came from Dick Rover, with a sigh. "Sometimes I wish all those happy days could be lived over again."

"When you think of those days, Dick, just think of what great times are in store for our boys," said Sam. "I only trust they have as good times as we had."

"I guess they'll know how to take care of themselves all right enough," was Tom Rover's comment. "But, just the same, we can't permit them to become too wild. Sending them to that private school in New York City doesn't seem to have done them so very much good, although, of course, I admit they are well educated for their age."

"I know where I'm going to send Jack when the proper time comes," answered Dick Rover.

"Where?" came from his brothers.

"I'm going to send him to Colby Hall, the military academy which our old school chum, Larry Colby, has opened. Larry sent me some of his literature some time ago; and I have heard from several people that it's already a first-class institution of learning—every bit as good as Putnam Hall."

"Well, if it's half as good as dear old Putnam Hall it must be some school," said Tom Rover. "And there's no reason why Larry Colby shouldn't be able to run a first-class military academy. He was a good scholar and a first-class cadet when he was at Putnam Hall."

"After Larry left Putnam Hall he went to travel in Europe,"

continued Dick. "Then he went through college, and immediately after that he joined the militia of New York State and there worked his way up until he now sports the title of colonel."

"Colonel Colby, eh? That's going some," was Tom's comment.

"His school is patterned after West Point, as was Putnam Hall, and I understand he has a West Point officer there to instruct the cadets in military tactics."

"Well, that's the sort of school our boys will need," answered Tom Rover. "The stricter it is the better it will be for them."

"I think it would be a good scheme to send them to Larry Colby's school," was Sam's comment. "As Larry knows us so well he would probably take an especial interest in our boys."

"Yes. But I wouldn't want him to show our lads any special favors," broke in Tom, quickly. "If the boys went there, I should want them to stand on their own feet, just as we did when we went to Putnam Hall."

"That's the talk, Tom! No favoritism!" cried Dick. "The only way to make a boy thoroughly self-reliant is to make him take his own part."

"If we are going to send them off to boarding school, they might as well go this Fall as any other time," remarked Sam Rover. "Have you any idea when the term at Colby Hall begins, Dick?"

"About the middle of September."

"It's the middle of August now. That would give us a full month in which to make arrangements and for them in which to get ready."

"Have you ever said anything to the twins about going to boarding school, Tom?" questioned Sam.

"Oh, yes. They understand that they are to go to some place sooner or later. Fred understands it, too, doesn't he?"

"Yes."

"And I told Jack only a short while ago that he must get ready to think of leaving home," put in Dick Rover. "Of course, it will be rather hard on the boys at first. They have never been away from us at all except the two weeks when they were out in that boys' camp."

"They'll have to get used to it, just as we got used to it when father went off to Africa and Uncle Randy sent us to Putnam Hall. Perhaps we had better tell them—"

Sam Rover broke off short as a series of shrieks in a high-pitched feminine voice issued from the pantry of the big farmhouse. An instant later a hired girl, followed by a middle-aged cook, came flying forth from the kitchen doorway.

"Oh, save me! Save me!" cried the hired girl, clutching her skirts tightly around her ankles, "Save me!"

"Oh, Mr. Rover! Mr. Rover! It's those dreadful boys! I won't stay here another minute!" screamed the cook, flourishing a big spoon in one hand and a dish-cloth in the other. "It's outrageous! That's what it is! I'm going to pack my trunk and leave this house right away!"

"What's the matter?" demanded Tom Rover, quickly.

"Are you hurt?" came anxiously from Dick.

"What have the boys done now?" questioned Sam.

"What have they done?" wailed the hired girl. "I just went into the pantry and opened the closet door and out jumped about a thousand mice at me!"

"Yes! and they are running all over the house!" broke in the cook savagely. "One of 'em ran right over my foot and tried to bite me! I'm going to pack my trunk and leave! I won't stay here another minute!"

Arthur M. Winfield

CHAPTER II

SOMETHING OF THE PAST

At the announcement of the hired girl that their sons had let loose in the farmhouse a thousand mice—more or less—the three Rover brothers looked at each other enquiringly.

"Another joke—and so soon!" gasped Sam Rover.

"That certainly is the limit!" broke out Dick Rover, as he started for the house.

"If I find Andy and Randy have been up to another trick right on top of this water-hose nonsense, I'll give them a tanning they won't forget in a hurry," added Tom Rover; and then he and Sam followed Dick up the back porch and into the kitchen.

To the readers of the former volumes in these two "Rover Boys Series," Dick, Tom and Sam Rover will need no special introduction. For the benefit of others, however, let me state that the sober-minded and determined Dick was the oldest of the three, with the fun-loving Tom coming next and sturdy Sam being the youngest. They were the sons of one Anderson Rover, who, when not traveling, made his home at Valley Brook Farm, in New York State, living there with his brother Randolph Rover and wife Martha.

While Dick, Tom, and Sam were quite young, and while their father was off exploring in the interior of Africa, the three Rovers had been sent to Putnam Hall Military Academy, where they had made a few enemies and likewise a host of friends, including a manly and straight-forward cadet named Lawrence Colby. After many adventures both at school and in various portions of the globe, they had graduated from Putnam Hall with honor and then entered Brill College.

At that time, Mr. Anderson Rover, who had long since returned from Africa, was not in the best of health. He had numerous business interests both in Wall Street, New York City, and in the West to take care of, and presently it was found necessary that Dick leave college and take charge of business matters for his parent. In this task Dick was soon aided by Tom, leaving Sam the only member of the family to graduate from Brill.

While at Putnam Hall the three Rovers had become acquainted with three charming girls, Dora Stanhope and her cousins, Nellie and Grace Laning. This acquaintance had ripened into loving intimacy; and when Dick went into business he took Dora Stanhope for his life-long partner. A little later Tom was married to Nellie Laning, and, after he had left Brill and joined his brothers in conducting their father's various business enterprises, Sam married Grace Laning.

With the aid of Mr. Anderson Rover and some others, The Rover Company was organized with offices on Wall Street, New York City. The company dealt in stocks, bonds, real estate, and other investments; and Dick was now president, with Tom secretary and Sam treasurer. The company had been prosperous from the start, although on several occasions enemies had done their best to give the concern a black eye.

When they were first married, Dick and his beautiful wife Dora had begun housekeeping in a cosy apartment in the metropolis, and they had presently been followed by Tom and Sam. But two years later the three brothers had a chance to buy a beautiful plot of ground on Riverside Drive facing the noble Hudson River, and on this they built three fine houses adjoining each other, Dick living in the middle house with Tom on one side and Sam on the other.

Before the happy young folks moved into the new homes, Dick and Dora were blessed with a little son, who later on was named John, after Mr. John Laning. Later still, this couple had a daughter, whom they named Martha, after Aunt Martha of Valley Brook Farm. Little Jack, as he was called in those days, was a wonderfully bright and clever lad with many of the clear-minded qualities which had made his father so successful in life.

About the time young Jack was presented with a baby sister, Tom and Nellie Rover came forward with twin boys, one of whom was named Anderson, after his grandfather, and the other Randolph, after his uncle. Andy and Randy, as they were always called for short, were exceedingly bright, each taking after his father, Andy always saying things that were more or less funny and Randy playing tricks whenever he got the chance. They were truly chips off the old block, and Tom knew it, although outwardly he professed to be ignorant of the fact.

"Those twins will be some boys when they grow up," was old Anderson Rover's comment, when the lads were less than five years old. "They're just as full of fun now as Tom ever dared to be."

"So they are," answered his brother Randolph. "My! my! what will they ever do with them when they get a little older?"

"I sha'n't mind," said Aunt Martha, her eyes beaming brightly. "That is, if they are really and truly as good-hearted as Tom has always been. He certainly was the worst of the lot when it came to playing jokes, but no lad ever had a better heart than Tom—not one!"

About the time that Tom began to boast about his twins, Sam and Grace came along with a beautiful little girl, whom they named Mary, after Mrs. Laning. About a year later the girl was followed by a boy, and this sturdy little chap was named Fred, after Sam's old school chum, Fred Garrison.

Living so close together, the four boys and the two girls were brought up almost like one big family. The girls were all but inseparable, and the boys could generally be found together, either studying, playing, or having a good time.

When the time came to set the children to studying, Martha and Mary were placed in a private school for girls located but a short distance from their homes. It was thought best, however, at the start to send the boys to a public school, and this was done. For three years matters went along very well, and during that time The Rover Company prospered far beyond the expectations of those in charge. But then Andy and Randy, becoming a little older, began to exhibit their talent for playing tricks, and usually they were seconded in these efforts by Jack and Fred. Once or twice all of the boys were reported by the school principal for this, and each time the lads were remonstrated with by their fathers in such a manner that, as young Andy expressed it, "it was far more comfortable to sit down standing up than it was any other way."

"I think I'll have to do something with those twins," said Tom Rover to his wife, after the boys had been reported for more tricks. "The school they go to doesn't seem to be strict enough." And thereupon he had sent the boys to a private establishment further uptown.

Jack and Fred had begged their parents that they might be allowed to do likewise; and at this private school the four cousins had been kept until the close of the Spring term the preceding June. To the credit of this school it must be said that the boys advanced rapidly in their studies. Their deportment, however, was apparently no better than it had been before, and as a consequence Tom Rover was more worried than ever, while Dick and Sam began to wonder secretly whether it would not be advisable to separate their sons from the mischievous twins.

One day Dick broached this subject to his offspring. At once young Jack set up a wild remonstrance.

"Oh, Dad! don't take me away from Andy and Randy and Fred!" he pleaded. "Why, we are just like brothers! I wouldn't know how to get along without 'em."

"But I'm afraid Andy and Randy are leading you into bad habits," returned Dick Rover.

"I don't think so, Dad. Anyway, I've heard folks say that Andy and Randy are no worse than their father used to be— and you never wanted to be separated from Uncle Tom, did you?"

At this question Dick Rover's face took on a sudden sober

look. "No; I never wanted to be separated from your uncle, that's true," he said. "But I tell you what we did used to do. When his pranks got too wild I and your Uncle Sam used to hold him in."

"All right then, Dad. I'll tell Fred about this, and we'll see what we can do towards holding in Andy and Randy;" and there, after some more talk along the same line, the matter was allowed to rest.

Young Jack was as good as his word, and during the remainder of that Spring term at the private school in New York City, Andy and Randy were as well behaved as could possibly be expected from two red-blooded lads.

It had been planned by the Rovers that the Summer should be spent by all the young folks and their mothers at Valley Brook Farm, the fathers to come down from time to time, and especially over the week ends. Since Dick, Tom, and Sam had become married the farm had been enlarged by the purchase of two hundred additional acres. The farmhouse, too, had been made larger, with the old portion remodeled, and a water system from the rapidly-growing town of Dexter's Corners, as well as electric lighting, had been installed. A telephone had been put in some years previous.

At first after their arrival at their grandfather's home, the four boys had been content to take it easy, spending their time roaming the fields, helping to gather the fruit, of which there was great abundance, and in going fishing and swimming. But then Andy and Randy had found time growing a little heavy on their hands, and one prank had been followed by another. Some of the tricks had been played on Jack and Fred, and they, of course, had done their best to retaliate, and this had, on more than one occasion, brought forth a forceful, but good-natured, pitched battle, and the fathers and the

Arthur M. Winfield

others present had had all they could do to hold the boys in check.

"I never saw such boys," was Mary Rover's comment to her brother Fred. "Why can't you behave yourselves just as Martha and I do?"

"Oh, girls never have any good times," answered Fred. "They just sit around and primp up and read, and do things like that."

"Indeed!" and Mary tossed her curly head. "I think we have just as good times as you boys, every bit; but we don't have to be rough about it;" and then she ran off to play a game of lawn tennis with her cousin Martha.

The time was the middle of August, and as the summer was proving to be an unusually warm one, all the older Rovers were glad enough to take it easy on the farm, they having earlier in the season been down to the seashore for a couple of weeks. Dick, Tom and Sam had each taken a week off at various times, and all managed to get down to the farm early every Saturday afternoon, to remain until Sunday night or Monday morning.

And it was late on a Saturday afternoon, when the ladies and the girls had gone to Dexter's Corners to do some shopping, and while the fathers were busy reading and writing, that the events occurred with which the present story opens.

As Dick Rover ran into the farmhouse he heard a slight scream coming from the sitting-room. The scream was followed by exclamations from two men, and then a wild thumping as if someone was hitting the floor with a cane.

"It's a mouse—several of 'em!" came in the voice of

Grandfather Rover.

"Oh, my! oh, my! wherever did they come from?" exclaimed old Aunt Martha.

"Never mind where they came from, I'll fix 'em," asserted old Randolph Rover, and then followed another thumping as he rushed around between the chairs and behind the sofa, trying to slaughter some of the scampering mice with his heavy walking stick.

"Where are they? Where are those mice?" demanded Tom Rover, giving a hasty glance around the kitchen.

"There is one—under the sink!" ejaculated his brother Sam, and catching up a stove lifter he let fly with such accurate aim that the unhappy rodent was despatched on the spot.

"I see another one back of the pantry door," said Tom Rover a moment later, and then made a dive into the pantry. Here, in a side closet, the door of which was partly open, he saw a broom and grabbed it quickly. Then he made a wild pass at the mouse, but the rodent eluded him and scrambled over the kitchen floor and into the sitting-room.

"Oh, dear! Oh, dear! Did you ever see so many mice?" came in a wailing voice from Aunt Martha. She had clambered up on a chair and stood there holding her dress tightly around her feet.

"It's another of those boys' tricks, that's what it is," asserted Grandfather Rover. "They ought to be punished for it."

"Yes. But we've got to get rid of these mice first," answered his brother.

Then Randolph Rover, seeing a mouse scampering across the side of the room, threw his walking stick at it with all his force. But his aim was poor and the walking stick, striking the edge of the table, glanced off and hit a fish-globe, smashing it to pieces and sending the water and the goldfish flying in every direction.

CHAPTER III

WHAT FOLLOWED ANOTHER TRICK

When the hubbub downstairs started the four Rover boys were up in their adjoining bedrooms partly undressed and in the midst of a couple of impromptu boxing matches, one taking place between Andy and Jack and the other between Randy and Fred.

"There, my boy, how do you like that?" cried Andy, as, dancing around, he managed to land a slapping blow on Jack's bare shoulder.

"Fine, child! fine!" retorted young Jack. "But not half as good as this," he continued, and, with a sudden spring, he landed one blow on Andy's chest and another on his shoulder which sent Tom's son staggering half-way across the bed.

"Hurrah! one man down! Now for the next!" cried Fred, and managed to land several blows in quick succession on Randy's shoulder.

But then the fun-loving twin came at him with a rush, sending him into a corner and on to a little table containing a number of books. As Fred went down the table did likewise and the books fell all over him.

Arthur M. Winfield

"Whoop!" roared Randy in his delight. "Down and buried!"

"But not dead," retorted Fred, promptly, and catching up several of the books he hurled them in quick succession at his opponent. One in particular caught Randy in the stomach, and down he sat with a suddenness that jarred the floor.

"Say!" exclaimed Jack, suddenly, and held up his hand, "this won't do at all. The folks downstairs will think we're pulling the house down over their ears. We'll have to slow up a bit. You know what our fathers said a little while ago."

"All right," returned Andy, promptly, as he arose to his feet. "After this we'll be as quiet as a thunder storm in a moving picture drama."

"That's the talk! Silence it is!" cried his twin; and then to let off a little extra steam he silently turned a cart-wheel across the floor, after which he proceeded with his toilet making.

The boys were still minus their collars and ties when they suddenly realized that something unusual was taking place downstairs. They had closed the bedroom doors, but now all of them rushed out into the hallway.

"Great watermelons!" groaned Randy, and turned slightly pale. "I forgot all about 'em!"

"About what?" chimed in Jack.

"You don't mean the mice?" demanded Andy.

"Yes, I do!"

"What mice?" questioned Fred.

"The mice I caught under the flooring of the old wagon house yesterday," answered Randy.

"I thought you put them in a cage and drowned them in the brook."

"I was going to do that, but then I changed my mind and put 'em in a couple of boxes. I thought maybe I might have a chance to train 'em—just like those mice we once saw in a show."

"Where did you put those boxes?" demanded Andy, quickly.

"I—I—didn't know exactly what to do with 'em, so—I—I—put 'em on the shelf in the pantry downstairs," faltered the twin.

"Great catfish, Randy! you've got us into a fine mess!" broke in Fred.

"Coming right on top of that trouble with the water-hose!" added Jack, ruefully.

After that there was a moment of silence, the four cousins gazing at each other uncertainly. Then Randy drew a long breath.

"Well, I'm going downstairs to see what's doing," he declared. "If I've got to suffer for this, I might as well see the fun."

"I'm going down, too," responded his twin, and side by side they ran down the stairs, with Jack and Fred close at their heels.

Perhaps it was poetic justice that Randy, who had been the

Arthur M. Winfield

cause of this commotion, should suffer the worst for it. Hardly had he put his foot in the lower hallway of the farmhouse when a mouse, scampering from a nearby doorway, made directly for him. The boy made a wild jump to step on the rodent, missed his footing, and came down flat on his back. He landed directly at the foot of the stairs, and his brother, being unable to stop, fell on top of him.

"Hi! Get off of me!" gasped the unfortunate youth. "What do you want to do—crack my head open?"

"Next time you go down, give a fellow warning," retorted his brother, scrambling to his feet; and then the two boys, with Jack and Fred, entered the sitting-room, doing this just as their fathers came in from the direction of the kitchen and just when old Uncle Randolph made his unfortunate attack on the fish-globe.

"Hello! look at the fish on the floor," exclaimed Jack. "What's the matter, Grandfather? Did the mice upset the globe?"

"No. I did that, trying to hit one of the pesky creatures," explained old Uncle Randolph. "We must kill them some way or they'll get all over the house, and then none of us will have any peace."

"I wouldn't care for a piece of mouse, anyway," remarked Andy, but in such a low tone that none of the older folks heard him.

"Everybody get a stick and go at those mice," commanded Dick Rover, and looked at the boys so sternly they all began to feel uncomfortable. "We've got either to kill them or drive them out of the house, otherwise the lady folks won't be able to sleep to-night."

"I'll get a poker and kill as many of 'em as I can," cried Randy, and ran out into the kitchen to do as he had mentioned.

The other boys, as well as their fathers, armed themselves with canes, umbrellas, and brooms, and for the next fifteen minutes there was a rapid and thorough search for all of the rodents. Several were driven outside through the open doors, while others were caught and slaughtered in various parts of the kitchen, the pantry, and the rooms adjoining. Then the goldfish were gathered up and put into another bowl of water and the bits of broken glass were removed.

"I'm awfully sorry, Uncle Randy, you broke the fish-globe," said Randy, contritely, "but I'm glad you saved the fish."

"Look here, young man, I want to talk to you—and to you, too!" cried Tom, sharply, and without more ado caught each twin by the arm and marched them into the library.

"Wow! I'm afraid Andy and Randy are in for it now," whispered Fred to Jack.

"Well, Randy certainly had no right to put those mice in the pantry," answered his cousin. "Just the same, I hope Uncle Tom isn't too severe with 'em."

"I don't see why Andy should be punished for this."

"Oh, they always stick together. You know that as well as I do."

"So I do. Isn't it wonderful how each is willing to share the blame with the other?" added Fred, with deep admiration.

Once in the library, Tom Rover shut the doors tightly and

Arthur M. Winfield

then faced his twin sons.

"Now then, I want the truth about this," he commenced sternly. "Where did those mice come from?"

"They came from under the flooring of the old wagon house," answered Randy. "I caught them there when the carpenters tore up the floor to put down the new one."

"And where did you put them?"

"I put 'em in a—er—a couple of boxes."

"Randy was going to keep the mice and try to teach 'em to do tricks, just the same as those mice we once saw in a vaudeville show," put in Andy, quickly, to do what he could to shield his brother.

"More tricks, eh?" was Tom's dry comment. "It seems to me that it is nothing but tricks lately. I suppose you placed the boxes in the pantry just so the mice wouldn't catch cold, didn't you?" he went on quizzically.

"No, sir. I—I—placed 'em there just for safekeeping," was the hesitating answer. "I didn't know that Lulu would disturb them."

"That's it, Dad. I'm sure Randy didn't want 'em disturbed."

"And what did you have to do with this, Andy?" demanded the father.

At this the boy addressed had nothing to say.

"He had nothing to do with it, Dad," answered Randy. "I got the mice and put 'em in the two boxes. I s'pose it wasn't just the right thing to put 'em in the pantry, but I give you my word I didn't think they'd be upset the way they were and be sent running all over the house. If Lulu hadn't touched the boxes, the mice would be there yet."

"Perhaps," answered Tom Rover, dryly. "Just the same, I think you placed the boxes there hoping that Lulu or the cook would have curiosity enough to see what they contained. As it is, your actions have upset the whole house, brought on the destruction of the fish-globe, and the cook is so upset that she has threatened to leave."

"Oh, she won't leave, Dad. She likes her big wages too well," remarked Andy, quickly.

"I don't know about that, Son. Nobody is going to stand for your tricks much longer. They are getting altogether too numerous." Tom continued to look as stern as possible. "I've got to take both of you in hand, and that is all there is to it. You are growing wilder every day. Something has got to be done. Now you go right upstairs and finish dressing, and don't dare to let me hear of any more tricks being played for the rest of this day, otherwise I'll not only give you a sound thrashing, but I'll cut off your spending money and do several other things that you won't like;" and, thus speaking, the father of the twins opened the door to the hall and shoved them both out towards the stairs with more force than they had felt for some time. The two lads lost no time in retiring to their bedroom.

"Say, Randy, I think you got off rather easily," remarked Andy, when they were alone.

"I think so myself," was the quick response. "I thought Dad would be so mad that he would give me one everlasting licking."

"Say! how did you make out?" questioned Fred, eagerly, as he came sneaking in, followed by Jack.

"You don't look as if you had suffered very much," was Jack's comment. "I thought you'd come out looking as if you'd been through a threshing machine."

What Randy and Andy had to tell was quickly related. At the conclusion, Jack, who being somewhat older than any of the others, was looked upon as something of a leader, shook his head thoughtfully.

"I guess we had better pull in our horns a little, for a while at least," was his conclusion. "My father was mighty mad, too, and so was Fred's. If we don't look out, we'll all get in wrong. They didn't like that wetting business to start with."

While the boys were finishing their toilet and discussing the matter, their fathers were doing what they could to set matters to rights downstairs, and to pacify their Aunt Martha and also the cook and the hired girl. The cook was particularly wrought up.

"It ain't the first time nor the second time nor the third time that them boys have played tricks on us," she declared. "It's been nothin' but one thing or 'nother ever since they came here—and last Summer it was the same way. The first thing you know, they'll be doin' somethin' awful, and some of us'll get hurt. I think I had better leave."

"If she leaves, I'll leave too," declared the hired girl.

"Don't think of leaving," said Tom Rover. "I'll take those boys in hand and see to it that they don't bother you any more. If they do the least thing, I'll pack them back to our house in New York." And after a little more talk he succeeded in mollifying the cook and the hired girl to such an extent that they went back to their work. Then the fathers of the boys withdrew once more to the library.

"I don't know how you feel about it," began Tom, after he had picked up his comic paper once more and then thrown it aside in disgust. "I begin to think that the best thing I can do is to pack those twins off to Colby Hall."

"I don't know but what I agree with you, Tom," answered Sam. "And if you do send them, I think Fred might as well go along."

"Yes; and Jack also," added Dick. "Those boys will never want to be separated, and I don't know that we could do better than to place them under Larry Colby's care, especially if we let Larry know just how wild they are apt to be and tell him to take them in hand."

"Yes; I'd want Larry to know all about them," answered Tom. "And I'd want him to give me his word that he'd keep a sharp eye on Andy and Randy and punish them severely every time they broke any of the rules. It's the only way to bring them up properly."

"All right then, Tom. If you think that way and Dick thinks the same, let's get right down to business and send a letter to Larry Colby to-night," said Sam.

"But what of the boys' mothers?" questioned Dick Rover. He knew that his wife Dora would grieve considerably over having young Jack leave home.

"We'll have to explain the situation to them and get them to agree," answered Tom, firmly.

CHAPTER IV

JACK IN WALL STREET

"Just to think, Jack! a week from to-day we'll be on our way to Colby Hall Military Academy."

"Yes, Fred. Doesn't it seem wonderful? I do hope we'll find the school to our liking," returned Jack, with a serious look on his face. "It would be too bad to go to some punk school."

"Oh, you can be sure that the school is all right; otherwise our fathers wouldn't have picked it out for us," broke in Andy. "They know what a good military academy is. Didn't they go to that famous old Putnam Hall?"

"I wish we could have gone to Putnam Hall," added Randy. "From what dad has told me, it must have been one dandy school."

"Well, we can't go to something that ain't," answered his twin with a grin. "Putnam Hall doesn't exist any more. When it burnt to the ground, Captain Putnam felt too old to have it rebuilt, and so he settled with the insurance companies and retired."

"Gee! but won't we have dandy times if that school is what

we hope for?" cried Andy. "We'll make things hum, won't we?"

"Right you are!" came in a chorus from the others. And then, in sudden high spirits, the boys began to wrestle with each other, ending up with something of a pillow fight in which not only pillows but also bolsters and numerous other articles were used as missiles.

After a never-to-be-forgotten vacation at Valley Brook Farm, the boys, along with their sisters and their parents, had returned to their homes in New York City. The Summer was almost at an end, and schools all over were opening for the Fall and Winter term.

It had been no easy task for Dick, Tom, and Sam Rover to convince their wives that it would be best to send the boys to some strict boarding school instead of to the private school which they had been attending in the metropolis. Gentle Dora Rover had cried a little at the thought of having her only son Jack leave home, and Grace Rover had been affected the same way at the thought of parting from her only boy Fred.

"But both of you will be better off than I shall be," had been Nellie Rover's comment. "Each of you will have a daughter still at home, while both of my twins will be gone and I'll have nobody;" and her eyes, too, had filled with tears.

But with it all, the mothers were sensible women, and they agreed with their husbands that the boys needed to be placed under strict discipline and that this was not possible at the school which they had been attending.

"That school is altogether too fashionable," had been Dick Rover's comment. "They make regular dudes of the pupils

Arthur M. Winfield

and they think more of high collars and neckties and patent-leather shoes than they do of reading, writing and arithmetic. Now, I want Jack to get a good education and I want him to learn how to behave himself while he is getting it." And so, after several communications had passed between the Rovers and Colonel Lawrence Colby, it was settled that the boys should be enlisted as cadets at Colby Hall.

"Cease firing!" cried Jack, when there came a lull in the pillow fight. "The first thing you know somebody will come in here and we'll be in hot water again." The boys were up in Jack's bedroom, and all of their mothers were downstairs, talking over the question of the wardrobes the lads were to take along to school.

"All right, Commodore," answered Andy, gaily. "Out of the trenches, boys; the war is over!"

"Suits me," panted Randy, who was all out of wind from his exertions. "Melt the cannons into telephones and send messages to the girls that the soldier boys are coming home," and at this remark there was a short laugh. Then all the boys proceeded to make themselves comfortable in various attitudes around the bedroom.

"Say! I'm glad of one thing," remarked Fred; "and that is, we won't be utter strangers at Colby Hall. Spouter Powell will be there and so will Gif Garrison."

It may be as well to explain here that Spouter Powell, whose real first name was Richard, was the son of the Rovers' old friend, John Powell, commonly called Songbird. Richard Powell did not seem to have much of his father's ability to write verse, but he did have a great fondness for making speeches, whence had come his nickname of Spouter.

Gifford Garrison, always called Gif for short, was the son of the Rovers' old schoolmate, Fred Garrison, after whom Fred Rover had been named. Gif was a big, strong youth who doted on athletic sports of all kinds. Both Gif and Spouter had visited the Rover boys on a number of occasions, and consequently all of the lads were well acquainted.

"Yes, I'll be glad to meet Gif and Spouter," returned Jack. "I like them both, even though Spouter gets pretty talky sometimes."

Just then there sounded downstairs a postman's whistle, and a minute later Martha Rover came upstairs.

"Here's a letter for you, Jack," said his sister, holding it out.

"Thanks," he returned, as he took the communication and glanced at it. "Why! what do you know about this? Here we were just talking about Gif and Spouter, and here is a letter from Gif now," he cried.

"Wonder what he's got to say," remarked Fred, and then, as he saw his cousin lingering at the doorway, he added: "Don't you want to come in, Martha, and join us?"

"No, thank you," she returned. "I'm going out with Mary. We're going to buy some things for you boys to take along when you go to that boarding school."

"Oh, I know what those will be," burst out Andy, gaily. "Pink neckties with yellow dots, or nice red socks with blue rings around 'em."

"Oh, the idea!" burst out the girl. "What an eye for color you have!"

Arthur M. Winfield

"Well, maybe it was blue socks with red rings around 'em," went on Andy, innocently; "and maybe the pink neckties will be plain yellow."

"Oh, Cousin Andy! I think you're just the worst ever!" shrieked Martha, and then ran downstairs to join those below.

In the meantime, Jack had torn open the letter and was scanning it hastily.

"Don't be selfish!" burst out Fred, curiously. "If Gif has anything to say about that school, let us hear it."

"Sure. I'll read it out loud," answered his cousin.

The communication, which was a rather long one, was of the usual boyish type, and much of it was of no particular interest. Several paragraphs, however, may be quoted here.

* * * * *

"You will be interested to know that besides Spouter Powell there will be another boy here who may or may not join our set. The fellow's name is Walter Baxter, and he is the son of Dan Baxter, the man who, years ago, caused your father and your uncles so much trouble at Putnam Hall and other places. Baxter is very hot-tempered and willing to fight almost any time.

"When I get back to school I am going in for athletics, particularly football this Fall, and I hope some of you fellows will want to go into athletics, too, for it will make it more interesting to have some friends on the eleven. Spouter don't go in for that sort of thing. He likes to save his wind for talk."

* * * * *

"Hum! that's rather interesting," was Randy's comment. "I wonder if this Walt Baxter will try to make trouble for us like his father did for our fathers?"

"Well, if he does, I guess we can take care of him, just as our folks took care of his father," returned his twin.

"No use borrowing trouble," came from Fred. "I've heard from my dad that Mr. Dan Baxter has reformed and is now a first-class business man and is quite prosperous. It may be that while his son Walt is somewhat hot-tempered, he may still be a thoroughly good fellow. I wouldn't give a rap for a boy that didn't show some spirit once in a while."

On the following morning Jack was on the point of going over to Fred's house to return some books he had borrowed, when his father called to him.

"I want you to go down to our offices with me this morning, Jack," said Dick Rover. "I've got a package there that I meant to bring up for your mother. You can come right back with it."

"All right, Dad. I'll be with you in a minute," answered the son, and ran off to deliver the books and to let Fred, as well as Randy and Andy, know where he was going.

Jack's temperament was a good deal like that of his father, and, young as he was, he already took an interest in what was being done in the offices of The Rover Company. On more than one occasion he had begged his parent's permission to visit the place on Wall Street, and once had been granted a "look-in" at the Stock Exchange during one of its busiest sessions. That sight was one he had never forgotten.

When the Rovers had first opened up in Wall Street, they had taken possession of a set of rather shabby offices

Arthur M. Winfield

formerly occupied by another firm with which they had had various difficulties, the particulars of which were related in "The Rover Boys in New York" and "The Rover Boys in Business." Now, however, they occupied the entire fourth floor of another building in a much better location. There was a large general office and a counting room, and a private office for each of the three brothers. Their office help numbered about twenty; and when business was brisk, the place consequently was a decidedly busy one.

When the offices of The Rover Company were reached, Dick Rover brought out the package intended for his wife. It was quite a bundle, and not wrapped as well as it might have been.

"You'd better let the office boy put an extra string around that, Jack," said the father.

"Oh, that's all right, Dad. I can get it home just as it is. There won't be much of a crowd on the subway train going uptown this time of day."

Jack spent a few minutes in the offices, speaking to the office boy and to several of the clerks with whom he was acquainted, and then started off for home, the bundle under his arm. He came down by one of the several elevators to the lower corridor of the building, and there stood in the wide-open doorway, contemplating the bustle in the narrow street beyond. Wall Street is the financial heart of our nation, and the activity there during business hours is something tremendous.

As Jack stood with his bundle under his arm, his attention was suddenly attracted to what was going on close by, beyond several columns which formed a part of the entrance to the building. In a niche of the wall stood a peddler, a short, sallow-faced and hollow-eyed man, evidently of foreign birth, trying to sell some cheap wares displayed on a little three-legged stand which he had set up. In front of the peddler stood a tall, slim, overbearing boy, loudly dressed and wearing light-colored spats and gloves to match.

"You've got no right to plank yourself here!" cried the overbearing boy savagely. "You get out of here or I'll dump that trash of yours into the street."

"Please, Mister, I am a poor man," pleaded the peddler in very broken English. "Please, Mister, you buy somet'in'?"

"You get out, I tell you!" went on the tall youth with a very lordly air. "Get out, I tell you! You foreigners are all thieves! Get out of here!" And without further warning he caught the thin, little peddler by the shoulder and gave him such a shove that the man had all he could do to keep from falling and from upsetting his little stock in trade.

CHAPTER V

GETTING READY TO LEAVE

"The mean fellow!"

Such was Jack's exclamation as he witnessed the scene between the hollow-eyed little street peddler and the dudish, overbearing youth who had attacked him.

"Get out, I tell you!" repeated the overbearing boy, as the peddler straightened up and caught hold of his little stand to keep it from tumbling over. "I've a big mind to kick your stuff into the street for you."

"Let up there, you big boob!" cried Jack, and without stopping to think twice he leaped towards the other youth and caught him firmly by the arm.

The boy who had attacked the peddler had not expected such interference, and he whirled around greatly surprised, especially when he saw a boy smaller than himself confronting him.

"What—what do you mean by catching hold of me this way?" he stammered.

"Why can't you leave that poor peddler alone?" retorted Jack.

"What business is this of yours?"

"That chap wasn't doing any harm here so far as I can see. He's only trying to earn his living."

"See here, kid! this is none of your affair, and I want you to keep out of it," stormed the dudish-looking youth. "We don't allow those fellows around this building."

"Then you tell him to move on in a decent kind of way," returned Jack.

"I'll do as I please." The big boy turned again towards the peddler and made a motion as if to push both the man and his stand down, but, instantly, Jack caught hold of him again and pulled him back, shoving him in between two pillars of the building's entrance.

"You had better go on," said Jack to the peddler, and, evidently much frightened by what was occurring, the little man took up his stand and disappeared as if by magic in the crowd on the street.

"Say! you've got gall to interfere with me!" burst out the big youth, glaring at Jack. "I'll teach you a lesson;" and with a sudden move he pulled Jack's bundle from under his arm and threw it out into the street. "Now you go about your business and don't you interfere with me again."

To have the bundle belonging to his mother treated in that fashion made the young Rover's blood boil. He jumped at the big youth, and as the other aimed a blow at him he dodged and then caught his opponent by the ear.

"Ouch! Let go!" screamed the big youth in sudden pain, and then he landed a blow on Jack's shoulder and received a crack on the chin in return.

How far this encounter might have gone, it is hard to say, but at that moment, while a crowd was beginning to gather, there came a sudden interruption in the appearance of Jack's Uncle Tom, followed by his Uncle Sam.

"Hello! What does this mean?" demanded Tom Rover, as he stepped between the two boys.

"It means that I've got an account to settle with that young snip, Mr. Rover!" cried the big youth savagely and giving Jack a look full of hatred.

"Uncle Tom, that fellow is nothing but a brute," declared Jack.

"A brute? What do you mean?"

"He just attacked a poor little peddler who was trying to sell a few things from a stand here in the corner. He tried to knock the peddler down and upset his stand. I told him to stop and then he attacked me."

"Humph! Are you this boy's uncle, Mr. Rover?" asked the big youth, in surprise.

"I am, Martell."

"Then I want to tell you that he has no right to interfere with me," went on Napoleon Martell, uglily. "Those peddlers are always hanging around here and my opinion is they are all thieves."

"That fellow was no more a thief than you are," broke in Jack, sturdily.

"Ha! Do you mean to call me a thief?"

"Come, Jack, such talk won't do down here in Wall Street," remonstrated his Uncle Sam, who had listened closely to what had been said. Sam Rover, from a distance, had seen the bundle flung into the gutter and had picked it up. Both the wrapping and the string were broken, but the contents of the package seemed to be uninjured.

"If that kid is your nephew, you had better take him in hand," grumbled Napoleon Martell, and then, not wishing to have any more words with the two older Rovers, he broke through the crowd which had gathered and hurried up the street.

"Come into the building," ordered Tom Rover to Jack, for the crowd was getting denser every instant; boys and men who had been hurrying by stopped to find out what was the matter.

"I guess I'll have to go back to get that bundle tied up again," answered Jack. The encounter had excited him not a little. "Uncle Tom, that fellow seemed to know you?"

"Yes, I know that boy. His name is Napoleon Martell, although they call him Nappy for short. He is the son of Nelson Martell, one of our rivals in business, a man who occupies the floor above us in this building."

"I didn't know Nappy was much of a scrapper," was Sam Rover's comment. "I thought he was too much of a dude to fight."

"He certainly is a dude as far as appearances go," answered

Jack; "but he has the manner of a brute. I wish now I'd had the chance to give him a good licking," he went on heartily.

"You had better go slow when it comes to fighting," returned his uncle. "A fight seldom settles anything."

"Didn't you ever have any fights, Uncle Sam?"

At this direct question Sam Rover's face became a study while his brother Tom looked at him rather quizzically.

"Yes! I had my share of fights when I was a boy," admitted the uncle. "But, looking back, I think a good many of them might have been avoided. Of course, I expect a boy to take his own part and not be a coward. But a fight isn't always the best way to settle a difficulty."

Once back in the offices, Jack did not hesitate to tell his father about what had happened. In the meantime, an office boy rewrapped the bundle, securing it this time with a stout cord.

"I am sorry to hear about this trouble, Jack," said his father seriously. "I don't want you to grow up into a scrapper."

"But, Dad, I couldn't stand by and see that fellow abuse a poor little peddler like that," answered the son. "It wasn't fair at all! What right had that Nappy Martell to order the man away?"

"No right, that I know of. Jack, except that Mr. Martell owns some stock in the company that owns this building; but that would be a very far-fetched right at the best."

"I guess those Martells are all tarred from the same stick," was Tom Rover's comment. "The father is just as overbearing as the son."

"Do you know what I'm inclined to think?" remarked Sam Rover, as he walked over and closed the door to the outer office so that the clerks might not hear what was said. "I'm inclined to think that Nelson Martell is a good deal of a crook."

"And that's just my idea of the man, too," added Tom Rover. "What do you think, Dick?"

At this direct question the oldest of the three brothers pursed up his lips in concentrated thought.

"To tell the truth, I don't know exactly what to think," he answered slowly. "Some of the things that Nelson Martell is trying to put through are certainly rather shady. Still, they may be within the strict letter of the law, and if that is so it would hardly be fair to call the man a crook."

When Jack returned home, he, of course, told his cousins of his encounter at the entrance to the office building.

"It's a pity you didn't have a chance to give Martell one in the eye or in the nose," was Randy's comment. "Such a brute deserves to be hauled down a peg or two."

"Well, I rather think I gave his ear a pretty good twist," answered Jack, grinning.

"You ought to have made him pick up that bundle he flung into the gutter," added Fred.

"I couldn't do much of anything with the crowd gathering around. My! how the people do flock together when the least thing happens! If we had stayed there another minute or two, we might have had a thousand people around us."

With so many things to be thought of and done previous to the departure for Colby Hall, the subject of Nappy Martell was soon dismissed. All the boys were wondering what they had better put in their trunks and suitcases.

"Gee! I've got enough stuff planned out to fill five trunks," declared Randy. "I want to take all my clothing, and my fishing outfit, and my football and baseball togs, and my gym suit, and I'd like to take along my dumbbells, and my physical culture exerciser, and maybe a shotgun, and that favorite paddle of mine, and—"

"And about five thousand other things," finished his twin. "I'm in the same boat. But we've simply got to cut down and take only the things that are actually necessary."

"We won't need any baseball things during this term," declared Jack. "The Fall is the time for football—not baseball. And say! we don't want to forget our skates. There's a river up there and also a lake; so if the winter gets cold enough there ought to be some dandy skating."

"Yes. And if the lake is large enough there ought to be a chance for some ice-boating," added Fred.

At last, with the aid of their parents, the four boys got their trunks and suitcases packed. They were to leave home for Colby Hall on Wednesday morning, and on Tuesday evening their folks gave them a little send-off in the shape of a party given at Dick Rover's residence. At this gathering many of their boy friends were present, as well as a number of girls along with Mary and Martha. All of the young folks had an exceedingly pleasant time, which was kept up until midnight.

"And now for Colby Hall!" exclaimed Jack, after the party had come to an end.

"That's it," returned Fred. "Colby Hall and the best times ever!"

"So say we all of us!" came from the twins.

Arthur M. Winfield

CHAPTER VI

ON THE TRAIN

"Ready?"

"I've been ready for the last half hour."

"So have I. Come on, if we're going to catch that train."

"Yes, boys, you don't want to miss the train," came from Mrs. Dick Rover. She gazed at Jack fondly. "Oh, dear! how I hate to have you go!"

"And how I do hate to see Fred leave!" sighed Mrs. Sam Rover.

"And my twins!" murmured Tom's wife. "I suppose they'll be getting into all sorts of mischief at that boarding school."

"Oh, Ma! we're going to be regular little lambs there," declared Andy.

"Just you wait and see what fine records we send home," added his twin.

"The automobiles are waiting, boys," broke in Dick Rover.

"Come. The train is due to leave in twenty minutes, and you know how crowded traffic is around the Grand Central Terminal."

There were hasty good-byes, a number of kisses and words of cheer, and then the four boys left their mothers and the girls and ran down to where two automobiles were standing at the curb. The twins and their father leaped into one, and Jack and Fred and their fathers into the other, and in a moment more the two machines were gliding down Riverside Drive on the way to the Grand Central Terminal at Forty-second Street.

It was a perfect autumn day, and all four of the lads were in the best of spirits. To be sure, the fact that they were leaving home to be gone for several months sobered them a trifle; but all were eager to find out what was in store for them rather than to give thought to what had been left behind.

As might have been expected, there was a perfect jam of automobiles and carriages in the vicinity of the Terminal, and as a consequence the lads had barely time to get aboard the train which was to carry them to Haven Point, the town on the outskirts of which Colby Hall was located.

"Take care of yourselves!" cried Dick Rover.

"Learn all you can," added his brother Sam.

"And go slow on mischief," warned Tom.

"We'll remember everything," came in a chorus from the four boys; and then, as they waved their hands to their parents, the long train pulled out of the big, gloomy station and the trip to the boarding school was begun.

Haven Point was located in the heart of New England, so that the boys had a ride of several hours ahead of them. They had seats in a parlor car, two on one side and two on the other, and they proceeded without delay to make themselves comfortable, the porter aiding them in disposing of their handbaggage.

"Good-bye to old New York!" cried Jack. "Won't we have a lot of things to talk about when we get back!"

"I'm just crazy to see Colby Hall, to find out what it really looks like," said Andy.

"That picture we had of it looked pretty good," was Fred's comment. "But, of course, you can't always tell by a picture."

"Not much!" vouchsafed Randy. "A building may look all right enough in a picture and still be about ready to tumble down."

The boys had left home in the middle of the forenoon, and expected to have their lunch on the train before reaching Haven Point.

"When lunch time comes I'm going to fill up," declared Andy. "No telling what sort of grub we'll get at the Hall."

"Father said they used to have first-class eats at Putnam Hall," declared Fred.

"Not always!" cried Jack. "At one time, while Captain Putnam was away, the food got so bad there that the cadets rebelled and left the school."

"Oh, that was before our fathers went to Putnam Hall," answered Randy. "I heard about that, too. But while our fathers were there, the food was very good, indeed."

After about half an hour's ride the train halted at a station, and among the passengers to get aboard were two youths with suitcases.

"Hello! what do you know about this?" cried Jack, surprised. "If there isn't Spouter Powell! I wonder what he is doing down here. He doesn't live in this town."

"And look at the fellow who is with him!" burst out Fred. "Did you ever see such a fat chap in your life?"

"Oh, say! I'll bet I know who that fellow is," declared Randy. "It must be Spouter's friend, Will Hendry. Spouter told me about him. They call him Fatty."

"And he fits his name," declared Randy. "Here they come now. They must have seats in this car."

Spouter Powell, a tall, thin youth with a mass of wavy, black hair overhanging his forehead, and wearing a small cap well back on his head, strode forward towards them. Behind him came the fat youth, struggling with a suitcase and puffing audibly.

"Hello, you Rover boys!" sang out the son of Songbird Powell, cheerfully. "I thought you might be on this train."

"Glad to see you, Spouter. How are you?" returned Jack, grasping his hand cordially. "Got a little friend with you, I see."

"Exactly! My chum, Will Hendry. Fatty, these are the Rover boys. This is Jack, this is Fred, and these two little innocent lambs are the twins, Andy and Randy."

"Glad to know you," came from all, and a general hand-shaking followed.

It was found that the new arrivals had two seats at the other end of the parlor car; but there were other seats vacant near the Rover boys, and an exchange for these was quickly made through the Pullman conductor.

"Say! they don't make you pay extra fare, do they?" queried Andy, as he looked at Fatty Hendry doing his best to squeeze into one of the chairs.

"Not yet. But I don't know what I'm coming to," puffed the stout youth. "Seems to me I'm taking on about a pound a day," he added, dolefully.

"Maybe you eat too much," suggested Randy, "Why don't you cut down on your victuals?"

"Eat too much!" puffed Will Hendry. "I don't eat half as much as some of you slim fellows. Why, Spouter here eats twice as much as I do!"

"Yes. But see the exercise I take," answered Dick Powell. "I walk at least five miles to your one. And I spend lots of time in the gym, too—something that you cut out entirely."

"Well, what would I be doing in the gym?" demanded the fat youth. "If I got up on the rings or the bars, I'd pull the whole blamed business down to the ground," and at this remark there was a general snicker.

Spouter Powell explained that he had been visiting Will Hendry, who lived in the town where the two had boarded the train. He had been at Colby Hall ever since its opening, and he had much to tell about the school and those who attended it.

"Oh, I'm sure you'll like it," declared Spouter, growing eloquent. "It's so delightfully situated on a hill overlooking the river, and is surrounded by stately trees and a well-kept campus. The scene from the front is exceedingly picturesque, while to the back the woods stretch out for many miles. Soon, when the frost touches the leaves, the hues and colors will be magnificent. The sparkle of the sunlight glinting across the water—"

"Wow! Spouter is off again!" puffed Fatty Hendry. "I told you to be careful," he pleaded.

"I was only acquainting them with the beauties of Colby Hall," remonstrated Spouter. "When one comes to contemplate nature, it's necessary to understand what real harmony—"

"Exactly, exactly! Just so!" burst out Andy. "We understand what you mean, Spouter. But please remember the scenery is there—it won't move—and we'll have lots of time to look at it."

"Tell us about the boys who go there—and the teachers," broke in Randy.

"Yes. The teachers especially," added Fred.

"Is there any hard-hearted fellow—like that Josiah Crabtree our folks tell about?"

"We've got one fellow there—Professor Asa Lemm—that nobody likes," answered Spouter. "He's a language teacher. They say he was once quite well off, and he constantly laments the loss of his wealth."

"And being poor now, he tries to take it out on every pupil who comes under him," finished Fatty Hendry. "Oh, Asa is a lemon, believe me!"

"Well, you know what lemons grow for," commented Andy, mischievously. "They are raised to be squeezed."

"And maybe we'll have to squeeze Mr. Asa Lemm—the lemon," added his twin.

"Then all the other profs are perfectly good fellows?" questioned Jack.

"Oh, yes! Captain Dale, our military instructor, is one of the nicest men I ever met, and so are Professors Grawson and Brice. The others don't seem to cut much ice one way or the other."

"Tell us something about the cadets."

"Any bullies there?" queried Fred.

"Yes; we've got one bully all right enough," answered Spouter. "Slogwell Brown is his name, but everybody calls him Slugger. He's from the country, but he thinks he knows it all and is very overbearing. You've got to keep your eye open for Slugger or you'll get into trouble sure."

"Thanks. I suppose we'd better give Mr. Slugger Brown a wide berth," remarked Fred, dryly.

"I don't think I'll let him ride over me," answered Jack, determinedly.

"Then, there is Walter Baxter. He isn't a half bad sort, although he's pretty hot-tempered. He had a room directly opposite Ned Lowe, who plays the mandolin and is quite a singer. About sixty of the old scholars are coming back, and then there will be quite a bunch of new fellows—not less than twenty, I've been told."

"Gif Garrison wrote to us and spoke about football," went on Jack. "I suppose they have some pretty good games up there?"

"Sure. We always have our regular eleven and a scrub eleven, and, besides that, we have two or three games with rival schools. Gif was at the head of the football eleven last season, and I suppose he'll be at the head this year, although Slugger Brown would like that place."

So the talk ran on, the Rover boys gaining quite a little information concerning the school to which they were bound. Then the porter came through the car announcing the first call for lunch.

"Say! let's go and have something to eat," cried Will Hendry, struggling to his feet.

"I thought you were going on a diet," remarked Andy, mischievously.

"Sure. But I'm going to have something just the same," answered the fat boy. "Come on if you are going to the dining car. If you wait too long, you won't be able to get a seat."

"My! I shouldn't think he'd want anything to eat for a month," whispered Fred to Spouter.

"Don't you believe a word of what Fatty says about cutting down on his food," returned the other in a low voice. "He eats just as much as anyone. That's what makes him so fat."

Possessed of the full appetites of growing boys, the Rovers were not loth to follow the fat youth and Spouter into the dining car, which, to their surprise, was almost full.

"We'll have to have a table for four and another table for two," remarked Jack to the head waiter. "Do you think you can find that many places?"

"Come this way," was the reply; and the party of six started for the other end of the dining car. They were about to take the seats assigned to them by the head waiter, when a very fussy man, accompanied by another man, pushed forward to crowd in at one of the vacant tables.

"Say! that's pretty cheeky," declared Randy. "Now I don't know where we are going to sit."

"I'll fix you up on the other side of the car," said the head waiter. The appearance of the boys had rather pleased him, while he did not like the actions of the fussy man and his companion at all.

Spouter and his fat chum were behind the Rovers, so they did not see the face of the fussy individual who had deprived the lads of one of the seats. They sat down on the other side of the aisle, and the Rover boys spread themselves around as best they could.

Fred and Jack had just sat down and Randy was doing likewise, when one of the waiters came through the swaying car carrying a tray filled with eatables. Suddenly the car gave an extra lurch, and Andy was thrown up against the waiter in such a manner that the tray tilted from the colored man's hand, and an instant later the contents of a large platter containing a broiled steak with some French-fried potatoes was deposited over the neck and shoulders of the fussy man in the seat near by.

"Oh!" roared the man, starting up in great anger. "What do you mean by this? What do you mean, I say?" he shrilled.

At the sound of this voice, Spouter Powell and Fatty Hendry looked up in sudden wonder. Then, as some of the Rover boys commenced to laugh over the mishap, Spouter clutched Jack by the arm.

"That man is Professor Asa Lemm!" he whispered.

Arthur M. Winfield

CHAPTER VII

A SCENE IN THE DINING CAR

"You don't mean it!" gasped Jack. "The lemon of a professor we were just talking about?"

"That's it!"

"Then I'm afraid Andy has gotten himself into trouble right at the start."

"It wasn't his fault. It was the lurching of the train did it," put in Fred.

"Just the same, I'd hate to be in your cousin's shoes," was Fatty Hendry's comment.

In the meanwhile the waiter, by a lightning-like move, had managed to save the broiled steak from slipping to the floor of the dining car. He now had it on the platter, but the French-fried potatoes were scattered in all directions.

"What do you mean, I say?" repeated Professor Asa Lemm in a loud, harsh voice.

"Scuse it, boss," answered the waiter humbly. "'Twas the

swingin' o' de car what done it. Besides, one o' dem passengers knocked agin my arm."

"I think it was that boy's fault quite as much as the waiter's," came from the man who was accompanying Professor Lemm.

"I couldn't help it," answered Andy. "The car gave such a sudden lurch that I was almost thrown off my feet."

"We'll fix this all up, sir," broke in the head waiter, coming to the front. "Take that steak back to the kitchen and bring some more potatoes," he added to the waiter. "I am glad to say it hasn't mussed you up very much;" and he handed the professor a fingerbowl full of water and an extra napkin.

A number of passengers had witnessed the accident and were smiling broadly. Spouter and Fatty Hendry were also on a broad grin, but their faces took on a sudden sober look when they found Asa Lemm's gaze directed toward them.

"Ha! so you are here," was the teacher's comment. "What business have you to laugh?"

"Excuse me, Professor Lemm, I—I—didn't—er—mean anything," stammered Spouter.

"Sorry it happened, very sorry," puffed Fatty.

"Is this young man traveling with you?" demanded Asa Lemm, suddenly, as he looked from Spouter and Fatty to Andy.

"Y—yes—sir," answered the son of Songbird Powell.

"Hum! Is he bound for the Hall?"

Arthur M. Winfield

"Y—yes—sir."

"Indeed? Then perhaps I'll see all of you later," muttered Asa Lemm; and after that did what he could with the aid of some water and a napkin to remove the traces of the accident from his person. In this he was aided by the head waiter, who was profuse in his apologies over what had occurred.

"I'm afraid you've got yourself into a pickle, Andy," whispered his twin, when the latter had taken his seat at the table.

"I don't care. I didn't mean to do it. It was an accident. Besides that, I think the waiter was as much to blame as I was."

"You'll never make old Lemon believe that," returned Spouter.

"Spouter's right about that," puffed out Fatty. "Once Asa Lemm gets down on a boy—good night!"

"I wonder who the man with him is?" questioned Spouter.

"Maybe it's a new teacher," vouchsafed Jack.

"I don't think so," returned Randy. "I heard both of them talking about some lawsuit and about money matters. Maybe the other fellow is a lawyer."

"I guess you're right," said Spouter. "As I told you before, old Lemon used to be worth a lot of money. Since he lost it he has been having one lawsuit after another trying to get some of it back. Most likely the other fellow is his lawyer." And in this surmise Spouter was correct.

The accident had sobered all the boys, consequently the lunch was not near so lively as it might otherwise have been. Still the irrepressible Randy could not hold back altogether, and he got what little sport he could out of it by putting some red pepper on Fatty's last mouthful of pie. He used a liberal dose, and the pie had scarcely disappeared within the stout youth's mouth when the boy began to splutter.

"Ug—ug—ugh!" came from Fatty as he made a wry face. "What pie! That last mouthful was like fire—full of pepper!"

"I thought the pie was rather hot," answered Randy, coolly.

"Hot! It's nothing but pep all the way through!" roared the fat boy. "Wow! let me have some water!" and he gulped this down so hastily that he almost strangled, the tears running down his cheeks. The other boys set up a laugh.

The boys had had some celery served with their lunch and several stalks which were not particularly good still remained in the dish on the table. When the boys were ready to leave, Professor Asa Lemm and his companion were still at their table discussing the particulars of a coming lawsuit.

"I'll give 'em something to remember us by anyhow," whispered Andy to the chums when the party had arisen to leave the dining car; and before any of the others could stop him he took up the stalks of celery and on passing Asa Lemm dropped them in the professor's side pocket, leaving the tops dangling outside.

"Gee! but you're some funny boy," chuckled Fatty, gazing at Andy in admiration. "I wish I could think of things like that to do."

"You'll think of 'em some day—when you get thin," returned

Arthur M. Winfield

Andy, encouragingly. "You see, I wanted to give him a bouquet to remember me by;" and at this remark there was a general snicker. Two or three of the passengers in the car had noticed Andy's action and all were smiling broadly over the incident.

"If he ever finds out who did that, he'll be down on you worse than ever," declared Jack, when the boys were once more in the chair car.

"Oh, well, what's the difference?" returned the light-hearted Andy. "I'd just as lief be shot for a mule as for a hoptoad."

"I suppose he's going on to the Hall," remarked Spouter. "If he is, I hope he doesn't get into the auto-stage with us."

"If he gets in the auto-stage, we might hire a jitney," suggested Fatty. "There are six of us, and we could get one of the jitneys to take us over to the Hall, baggage and all, for half a dollar."

A little later the train made a stop of several minutes at quite a large city. The boys were tired of sitting still and were glad enough to go out on the platform to stretch their legs. Here they saw Professor Lemm and his friend leave the train and walk up the main street of the place.

"Hurrah! we won't be bothered with him any more on this trip," declared Spouter.

"Look!" cried Randy, suddenly, pointing to the two men; and as the boys gazed in that direction they were just in time to see Asa Lemm pull the stalks of celery from his pocket and throw them in the street. His whole manner showed that he was much disgusted.

"And to think he has thrown away your beautiful bouquet, Andy," lamented Fred.

"Never mind, Fred; we have to get used to keen disappointments in this life," groaned Andy.

"Won't he be coming back?" questioned Fatty.

"I don't think so—he won't have time," answered Jack; "here comes the conductor now."

"All aboard!" shouted the conductor at that moment, and the boys had to hurry in order not to be left behind. Then the train pulled out of the station and the journey was continued.

"We certainly ought to have some dandy times," said Jack to Spouter, as the train sped along. "I suppose your father has told you of all the good times our folks had when they went to Putnam Hall and Brill College."

"Yes, Jack. That is, he has told me about a good many things. Of course I don't suppose he told me about some of the tricks they played."

"Well, I've heard from father and from my Uncle Sam that my Uncle Tom was playing tricks almost continually."

"Then Andy and Randy come by their fun-making naturally."

"They sure do! And what do you suppose the folks at home expect me to do?" went on Jack, seriously. "They expect me to hold those twins in. Why! a fellow could no more do that than hold in a pair of wild horses. You've seen a little of what Andy can do. Well, his jokes aren't a patch to those Randy occasionally gets off."

"You don't say! Well, I'm not sorry. The last term at Colby Hall was rather slow. Now maybe we'll have some life;" and Spouter's face lightened.

While the boys had been at lunch the sky had darkened, and now the train rushed into a sudden heavy shower, the rain driving against the windows of the car in sheets.

"I don't like this much," said Fred, dolefully. "Maybe we'll get out at Haven Point in a regular downpour."

"Oh, this looks more like a local shower than anything else," answered Jack. "We may run out of it in a few minutes."

"Some rain, all right," remarked Randy, as the water continued to dash against the windows.

"Just look there!" cried Andy, pointing out. "Before it began to rain I noticed the automobiles on yonder road kicking up quite a dust. Now just look at the water and mud."

"We'll be at Haven Point in twenty minutes—that is, if the train is on time," announced Spouter, consulting his watch. "Too bad! Because I wanted you to see the beautiful scenery with which the school is surrounded. Oh! the woods are perfectly beautiful, and after a heavy rain the torrent of water coming down the river makes the outlook one of marvelous beauty. I have stood there contemplating the scene—"

"Turn it off, Spouter! turn it off!" broke in Fatty. "You promised me on your bare knees that you would stop spouting about nature this term—and here you start in the first thing!"

"Oh, you haven't any more eye for beauty than a cow," retorted Spouter, ruefully.

"Why abuse the cow?" questioned Andy, gaily. "A cow has an eye for beauty. Just you hold out a beautiful red apple to her and see if she hasn't;" and at this the others grinned.

Haven Point was still five miles away when the boys saw that the rain was letting up; but the ditches along the track, and the highways wherever they passed them, were filled with running water, showing that the downpour in that vicinity had been a severe one.

"Next station Haven Point!" called out one of the trainmen as he came through the car.

"Better get your bags ready," cried Spouter. "There may be other fellows going to the Hall, and we want to get good seats on the auto-stage if we can."

"All right. You lead on, Spouter," answered Jack; "we'll follow you."

In a few minutes more Haven Point was reached and the long train rolled into the little station. One after another the boys alighted, the porter helping them with their suitcases and gladly accepting the tips they offered.

Spouter headed for a large auto-stage drawn up on the opposite side of an open plot behind the station. As the Rovers and their friends started for the turnout belonging to Colby Hall, they noticed that several other boys had also left another coach of the train and were headed in the same direction.

"New fellows, like ourselves, I suppose," remarked Fred. "Let's get ahead of 'em."

"That's the talk!" exclaimed Randy. "Come on!" and he set

off on a run beside Spouter with the others at their heels.

The rain had been falling heavily at Haven Point just previous to the arrival of the train, and consequently the open place behind the depot contained numerous hollows of water and mud, around which the boys had to make their way as best they could. They were rushing along as fast as their handbaggage would permit, when they came up side by side with three other lads also bound for the stage.

"Look out there!" cried Jack as one of the strangers leaped into a puddle of water, splashing the mud right and left.

"Look out yourself!" cried the other youth, a big lad, much larger than any of the others.

"That's Slugger Brown—the bully I was telling you about," explained Spouter as he continued to run.

Directly behind Slugger Brown came another youth, loudly dressed in a checkered suit and a soft checkered hat to match. He was rather fastidious as to where he stepped, and with his eyes on the ground ran directly into Fred.

"Hi! look where you are going!" cried the youngest of the Rover boys, and then, to keep himself from slipping down, made a clutch at Randy's arm. This brought Randy around, and both he and Fred bumped into the elegantly attired youth.

"Stop that!" cried the stranger, and then, seeing a puddle directly in front of him, attempted to leap over it. But his foot slipped in the mud and down he went flat on his back with a loud splash.

CHAPTER VIII

AT COLBY HALL

"My! look at that!"

"Some tumble that, eh?"

"Why! he sent some of that water and mud over me!"

Such were some of the exclamations as the loudly-dressed youth went down in the puddle of water and mud.

He was flat on his back, and it took several seconds for him to turn over and get to his feet. The fall had attracted the attention of everybody making for the auto-stage excepting Spouter and Jack.

"Oh, my eye! you're certainly a sight to see," came from the biggest boy in the crowd, Slugger Brown.

"It wasn't my fault that I fell," retorted the unfortunate one. "Those fellows bumped into me and made me lose my footing," and he pointed to Fred and Randy.

"No such thing!" burst out Fred, indignantly. "You bumped into us first; and you only fell when you tried to jump across

Arthur M. Winfield

the puddle and your feet slipped."

"I say it's your fault!" spluttered the boy who had gone down. His hands were covered with mud and water and he stood there helpless, filled with rage.

"Take your handkerchief and wipe your hands off," advised Slugger Brown. He looked coldly at Fred and Randy. "If they tripped you up, they ought to have a licking for doing it."

"That's the fellow who's responsible," answered the boy who had fallen, and he strode up to confront Fred. "For two pins I'd smash you on the nose," he continued, hotly.

"You leave him alone!" broke in Randy, and doubled up his fists.

The boy who had gone down had expected Fred to back away; but the youngest Rover bravely stood his ground.

"Say! what's up back there?" queried Spouter, suddenly looking around to see why the other boys had not followed him to the auto-stage.

"Looks to me as if somebody was going to get into a fight," returned Jack. "See! one of those fellows just made a pass at Fred. Come on, this won't do!" and he ran back towards the crowd that was gathering.

The boy who had fallen had, indeed, made a pass with one of his dirty fists at Fred, but the latter had dodged the blow with ease and now he had the loudly dressed youth by the arm.

"You behave yourself!" he said sharply. "I didn't knock you down, and you know it! I'm sorry you got yourself all dirty, but it wasn't my fault."

"You fight him, and you'll fight me too!" broke in Randy. "If there is any blame in this it belongs to me as much as to my cousin."

By this time Jack had reached the group and pushed his way to the front. As he caught sight of the face of the boy who had fallen, he gave a quick exclamation.

"Well I never! Nappy Martell!"

"Do you know this fellow?" questioned Andy, quickly.

"I've met him before," was the reply. "He's Nappy Martell—the fellow I had trouble with in front of the office in Wall Street—the fellow who so mistreated that poor street peddler."

"Oh! So this is the same chap, eh?" broke out Randy. "No wonder he wants to fight with Fred. He's a regular scrapper, in spite of his fine clothes."

"What are you doing here?" asked Nappy Martell, curiously, as he looked at Jack. Then his gaze suddenly shifted to Fred and Randy. "Are you Rovers, too?"

"We are," was the quick response.

"Humph! No wonder you knocked me down. I suppose that fellow told you all about me?" and Nappy pointed to Jack.

"What's the use of quarreling about a little thing like a tumble in the dirt?" panted Fatty, who was almost out of breath because of his run towards the auto-stage. "Come on! let's get to the Hall and see who is there."

"I'm not anxious to fight," answered Fred, readily; "but I

don't like this fellow's talk."

"I'll talk as I please," blustered Martell. "And I'll fight, too, if I want to."

"That's the talk, Nappy!" came from Slugger Brown. "Don't let any new boys lord it over you. If you want to fight, go ahead."

"I owe these Rovers one," muttered the loudly dressed youth. "I had a run-in with this one in New York," and he pointed to Jack. "They are all of a kind—too fresh to live."

"There is no use of your talking that way, Martell," broke in Jack. "We didn't come here to scrap, but everyone of us can take his own part if it is necessary."

A perfect war of words followed, and the argument proved so hot that it looked as if there would certainly be a fight with Fred and Randy, and possibly some of the others, on one side, and Nappy Martell, Slugger Brown and one or two of their cronies who had come up on the other. But then came a sudden diversion as a heavily built and military looking man came from the main street of the town and walked towards them.

"Cheese it, boys!" came from one of the lads present. "Here comes Captain Dale. He'll report us all if he knows there's anything like a fight going on."

At the announcement that Captain Mapes Dale, who was the military instructor at Colby Hall, was approaching, the boys who had attended the academy the term previous fell back in alarm. They knew the captain to be a strict disciplinarian who abhorred fighting except in a military way.

"Well, boys, are you going up to the Hall?" said the captain pleasantly, as he came closer. The old pupils present saluted him and were saluted in return.

"Yes, sir," answered Spouter. And then before any of the others could speak he added: "Captain Dale, will you permit me to introduce some new scholars?" and thereupon he mentioned the Rover boys' names.

"Glad to know you," said Captain Dale, and shook hands all around.

In the meanwhile Nappy Martell had dropped somewhat in the background so that the military instructor might not notice the soiled condition of his clothing. Then one or two other new pupils were introduced, and the whole crowd made for the auto-stage.

The stage was a large affair, and Slugger Brown, Nappy Martell and some of their friends kept to the front end, leaving the Rovers and their friends together at the rear, the captain and a professor connected with the Hall seating themselves between the two factions.

"This row is only stopped for the time being," whispered Randy to Jack. "I think that fellow Martell is too ugly to let it drop."

"He's rather a big fellow to tackle Fred," returned Jack. "Why, he is even bigger than I am!"

"That's the way with most bullies," put in Fatty. "They don't feel like tackling a fellow of their size. They like to pick out little chaps."

"Oh, don't misunderstand me," returned the oldest of the

Rover boys. "Fred may be small, but he is very strong and wiry, and he knows how to take care of himself. But I shouldn't like to see any out and out fighting—at least not so soon. We don't want to get a black eye before we get settled down."

"That's the talk!" came from Andy. "I'd rather have some fun than have any fighting. I hope we'll find the other fellows at the Hall more pleasant than this Martell and that great big Slugger Brown."

"It's queer you didn't mention Martell to us on the train," remarked Fred.

"I thought he had left school," answered Spouter. "You see, he went home before the term closed last Spring, and I didn't know that he was coming back."

"He and Brown seem to be pretty thick," was Randy's comment.

"Yes; they were always together last term, they and a fellow named Henry Stowell. Stowell is a regular little sneak, and most of the boys call him Codfish on account of the awfully broad mouth he's got."

"Well, there's one thing sure," remarked Jack; "we'll all have to keep our eyes open for Martell, Brown and Company."

While on the train the Rover boys had learned that Haven Point was a clean and compactly built town containing about two thousand inhabitants. It was located at the head of Clearwater Lake, a beautiful sheet of water about two miles long and half a mile wide and containing a number of picturesque islands. At the head of the lake was the Rick Rack River, running down from the hills and woods beyond.

Up in the hills it was a wild and rocky watercourse containing a number of dangerous rapids, but where it passed Colby Hall it was a broad and fairly deep stream, joining the lake at a point where there were two rocky islands. The distance from the railroad station to the Military Academy was a little over half a mile, along a road branching off through the main street into a country highway bordered on one side by the river and on the other by a number of well-kept farms, with here and there a small patch of timber.

"There's the Hall!" exclaimed Spouter presently, after the auto-stage made a turn through a number of trees and came out on a broad highway running in a semi-circle around a large campus. "What do you think of the place? Looks rather fine, doesn't it?"

All of the Rover boys gazed eagerly at what was before them. They saw a large stone building, shaped almost in the form of a cross, the upper portion facing the river. It was three stories in height and contained not only the classrooms and mess hall of the institution, but also the dormitories for the boys. To one side was a small brick building which at one time had evidently been a private dwelling. This was now occupied by Colonel Colby and his family and the various professors. On the opposite side was a long, low, wooden building.

"That's our gym," explained Fatty. "You can go in there any time you want to, do a turn on the bars, and break your neck."

Down at the water's edge were several small buildings which, Spouter explained, were used for storing the boats belonging to the Hall and also as bathhouses. Behind the Hall were a stable and a barn, and also a garage. And still farther back were a vegetable garden and some farm fields, for Colonel Colby believed in raising as much stuff for the Hall table as possible.

"That's the Rick Rack River," explained Spouter, as they passed the stream. "We've some dandy times there swimming and boating."

"Don't you have skating in the winter?" queried Andy.

"Sure! And we have some great races, too."

In another moment the auto-stage drew up to the front door of Colby Hall, and one after another the boys and Captain Dale and the other teacher alighted.

"You new pupils may as well follow me right to the office," said the captain. "You can leave your suitcases in the hallway until you have been assigned to your rooms."

He led the way, and they followed through a large reception room and into an elegantly appointed office where Colonel Colby sat at a mahogany desk, writing.

"Some new pupils, Colonel Colby," announced the captain, and at once the colonel arose.

"So you are the Rover boys, eh?" he said, his face lighting up with pleasure. "I am certainly very glad to meet you. Of course you know that your fathers and myself were school-mates for many years?"

"Yes, Colonel Colby, we know that," replied Jack. "That is one reason why they sent us here."

"So I understand. I am proud to know that my old friends think so much of me," and the master of Colby Hall smiled broadly. "I am sure we are going to get along famously."

"It certainly looks like a nice school," remarked Andy, frankly. "I like it first rate."

"And so do I," added his twin.

"We hope to have some great times here," came from Fred.

Then one after another the boys were required to sign the register and answer a number of questions regarding their age and previous instruction, and the state of their health.

"I'll have Professor Brice assign you to your rooms," said Colonel Colby, after the questioning had come to an end. "He has charge of that matter so far as it concerns the older boys. The younger boys are under the charge of Mrs. Crews, the matron."

The master of the Hall touched a bell, and when a servant appeared requested that Professor Brice be summoned. The latter soon appeared, a young man evidently just from college. He was introduced to the boys, and then took them off to assign them their rooms.

"Hadn't we better get our suitcases?" suggested Jack.

"Yes; you might as well bring them along," answered Professor Paul Brice. "That will save another trip downstairs. You can give your trunk checks to me, and I will see that the trunks are brought up from the station and placed in your rooms to be unpacked. After you've unpacked them, they will be marked with your names and placed in the trunk room."

It took the boys but a minute to reach the end of the hallway

Arthur M. Winfield

where their suitcases had been left. Those of the twins were still there, and also that belonging to Jack; but Fred's was missing.

"Hello! what's become of my suitcase?" questioned the youngest Rover, anxiously.

"Maybe somebody carried it upstairs for you," suggested Jack.

All looked around the hallway and in the nearby rooms, but the suitcase could not be found.

"Well, I don't think you need to worry," said Professor Brice lightly. "There is no danger of thieves around here. Probably some boy picked up the suitcase by mistake."

"Maybe," returned Fred; but then he looked at his cousins and shook his head slowly.

"I guess you suspect Nappy Martell and his cronies," whispered Randy on the way upstairs.

"I do!" answered Fred. "I think they took that suitcase to play a trick on me."

CHAPTER IX

THE MISSING SUITCASE

In the letters sent to Colby Hall the Rover boys had requested that they be placed in rooms close to those occupied by Spouter Powell, Gif Garrison and their chums, and Colonel Colby had replied that he would do what he could for them in the matter, although many of the choicest rooms at the Hall had already been assigned to the old cadets.

"I can give you a choice of several rooms," said Professor Brice, as he led the way to the second floor of the school. "Come this way, please."

He took them down a long corridor and into a wing of the building.

"This is our hallway," whispered Spouter to Jack. "I guess you'll get pretty close to Gif and me after all."

Spouter and Gif had rooms numbered 19 and 21. Across the hall, Fatty had number 16. 18, 20 and 22 were as yet unassigned.

"I can give you these three rooms," announced Paul Brice.

"But what about the fourth?" queried Jack. "There are four of us, you see, and all these are single rooms."

"For a fourth room you might take the one next to that occupied by Powell on the other side of the hallway," answered the teacher.

"That might do," returned Fred. "But we would prefer to be together—especially as these rooms all connect."

"I think I can help you out if you want me to," came from Fatty, good-naturedly. "If Professor Brice is willing, I'll move over to number twenty-three, and that will give you four fellows numbers sixteen, eighteen, twenty, and twenty-two."

"Oh, we don't want to disturb you, although it's very kind of you to make the offer," remonstrated Jack.

"That's all right," answered Fatty. "I'd just as lief be next to Spouter. The room is just as good, and I know you four cousins would like to keep together." And so, after a little more talk, the matter was arranged.

"Now the question is: How are we going to assign these rooms?" came from Randy.

"I've got an idea," returned his twin.

"All right; out with it!" came from Fred. "I'd like to get settled so that I can make another hunt for my missing suitcase."

"Why not live here just as we live on Riverside Drive?" answered Andy. "Jack can take one of the middle rooms, with Fred on one side of him and Randy and myself on the other."

"You've solved it, Andy!" exclaimed Jack, and so without further ado the matter was settled.

"Now I'll institute a hunt for that missing suitcase," said Professor Brice after he had made a note of the room assignments. "Most likely some boy picked it up by mistake."

"If he did that, why didn't he leave his own suitcase behind?" queried Fred.

"I'll look it up. Don't worry," said the professor, and then hurried away, for there were many other matters demanding his attention.

The boys found the rooms small but pleasant. Each contained a single bed, a desk, and a chiffonier, and also a small clothing closet. In one corner was a bowl with running water, and each room contained two electric lights. All of the rooms had connecting doors, but these, for the most part, were kept closed, some of the pupils having their beds or chiffoniers in front of them.

"You see, you are permitted to arrange your room to suit yourselves," explained Spouter, "so some of the boys have them one way and some another. Some of the boys are even permitted to double up—that is, put two of the beds in one room and use the other room exclusively for dressing and studying."

"That's an idea," answered Randy. "Maybe Andy and I will do that." This plan was followed out by the twins, who used the last room of the four for a sleeping apartment and made of the other room a sort of general meeting place for all of the Rovers.

"Where does that Nappy Martell hold forth?" questioned

Fred of Fatty, while he was helping the stout youth transfer his belongings across the hallway.

"He and Slugger Brown and Codfish and that gang are all around the corner, on the main corridor," was the reply. "That is, Nappy was there last season. I don't know whether somebody else used his room after he left or not."

"It was room sixty," put in Spouter. "Slugger has sixty-two. I don't believe anyone went into sixty after Nappy left. You see, it was almost the end of the term and all the cadets were settled."

"I'm going to take a look around," answered Fred. "I can't do anything here anyway, with no suitcase and no trunk."

"I guess I'd better go with you," came from Jack. He did not wish to allow his cousin to interview the big, over-dressed youth alone.

Leaving the others to settle down in the rooms as best they could, Fred and Jack hurried through the hallway to the main corridor of the second floor of the Hall. Old cadets and new pupils were coming and going in all directions, and many were the glances of curiosity directed towards the Rovers.

"Gee! some of those fellows certainly look nifty in their uniforms," was Fred's comment.

"They look like the uniforms our folks brought home from Putnam Hall," answered Jack. "My father's old uniform is up in our storeroom now. I tried it on one day just for fun. They tell me they are patterned after the uniforms worn at West Point."

"There goes an officer," whispered Fred, as a tall youth went by with a sword dangling from his belt. "Look at the gold braid, will you? Isn't it swell?" he added, in deep admiration.

"I can see your finish, Fred," laughed his cousin. "If you stay here, you'll want to be an officer with a sword, and with lots of gold lace."

"I don't know about that," answered the youngest Rover, seriously. "I guess all the officers have to be big boys."

"Nonsense! Size has nothing to do with it. Why, some of the greatest military men in the world have been very small. Look at Napoleon, for instance."

"Well, I'll see about that later, Jack. Just now I'd rather get on the track of that suitcase."

It did not take the two Rovers long to reach that part of the corridor where was located the room formerly occupied by Nappy Martell. The door was open several inches, and Fred and Jack saw that three boys were present—Nappy, Slugger, and a small, round-faced youth with a particularly broad mouth.

"That little chap must be the sneak Spouter mentioned—the boy they call Codfish," whispered Jack.

"That was a good joke all right, Nappy," piped out the small cadet, as the Rovers came closer. "A fine joke all right all right!"

"You keep your mouth shut about it, Codfish," retorted Nappy Martell, quickly.

"Oh, I won't say a word, believe me!" returned the other quickly.

Arthur M. Winfield

Just then Slugger Brown peered out into the hallway and saw the two Rover boys. He looked somewhat startled, and immediately placed his hand over Nappy Martell's mouth.

"I want to see you, Martell," cried Fred without hesitation. "I want to know what you did with my suitcase."

"I don't know anything about your suitcase," growled the loudly dressed youth in surly tones.

"Yes, you do! You took it; and I want you to return it," answered Fred, boldly.

"See here! do you want a licking?" burst out the New York boy, as he doubled up his fists. "You deserve one for the way you tripped me up in that mud puddle. You say another word, and I'll give you what's coming to you," and his manner was very threatening.

"No use of fighting here, Nappy," remonstrated Slugger Brown. "Keep it until some time when you can meet him outside."

"I didn't come here to fight," answered Fred. "But I want my suitcase."

"I don't know anything about your suitcase. Who says I took it?" added Nappy Martell with sudden suspicion.

"I say you took it. There wouldn't be anyone else here to play such a trick on me. Now, you must hand it over!"

"You go on about your business!" roared the New York boy; and as Fred, followed by Jack, attempted to enter the room, he slammed the door in their faces and shot the bolt into place.

Fred was thoroughly angry, and if it had not been for his cousin he would have tried then and there to batter the door down. But Jack caught him by the arm and pulled him back.

"No use of creating a disturbance so soon," said Jack. "We'd only get into hot water, and maybe Colonel Colby would become so disgusted he would send us right home. If Martell took that suitcase, he won't dare to keep it, for that would be stealing. More than likely he'll sneak it back to you by to-morrow."

"He ought to have his head knocked off of him," muttered the youngest Rover. "Jack, I feel in my bones that that fellow is going to cause us a lot of trouble."

"I shouldn't wonder," was the answer. "Remember, Fred; he is as angry at me for the row we had down in Wall Street as he is at you over that mud-puddle affair."

"Oh, dear! And I thought everything was going to be lovely when we got here," sighed Fred.

There seemed nothing else to do, and so the two boys returned to where they had left the others. A little while later their trunks came in, and all spent an hour or more in unpacking these and stowing away the various articles brought along.

"You'll be measured for your uniforms to-morrow," announced Spouter. "And then, if the school has the right sizes on hand, you'll get them at once. Otherwise, they'll be made to order and you'll have to wait at least ten days for them."

"Oh, I hope they've got my size in stock!" cried Andy. "I'd like to see how it feels being a cadet."

Arthur M. Winfield

"Don't worry," answered his twin. "I guess we'll get enough of that before we leave Colby Hall. Remember, you've got to learn how to drill, and march, and shoot at a target, and all that."

"I think it'll be lots of fun," broke in Jack. "My father told me he liked that part of the life at Putnam Hall very much."

"We're pretty well filled up here, it seems to me," came from Fred, as he sat on his empty trunk surveying his surroundings.

"The men will come to take the trunks away in a little while," answered Fatty; and this proved to be so. With the trunks gone the boys had more room in which to move about, for which they were thankful.

"How about supper?" questioned Andy, presently, as a bell rang out sharply.

"We have supper at six o'clock sharp," returned Fatty, quickly.

"Last year we were at a table with Professor Grawson," put in Spouter. "He's a pretty nice man. I hope I get at his table again."

"Excuse me from getting at a table with a man like Professor Lemm," burst out Andy. "Gee! what will I do if they put me with him?" he continued dolefully.

"Well, you'll have to sit wherever you are placed," answered Spouter.

"And what do you care so long as you get enough to eat?" questioned Fatty.

But Andy shook his head. He thought if he were placed at the same table with Professor Asa Lemm, it would be an actual hardship.

CHAPTER X

GETTING ACQUAINTED

"I don't see him anywhere," remarked Andy, as he and his cousins approached the mess hall of the school.

The cadets were entering in little groups of twos and threes, for as yet the regular term at Colby Hall had not begun. With the real opening of the school, the cadets would have a dress parade previous to dining and would then stack their arms outside and march in in regular order.

"Who are you talking about?" questioned Fred.

"Professor Asa Lemm. I don't see him at any of the tables."

"Maybe he didn't come to the Hall to-night. He might have had quite some business to transact with that man who left the train with him."

As there were more tables than professors, some of the boards were presided over by the senior cadets. There was a little confusion, due to the entrance of so many new pupils, and then the Rovers were assigned to a table presided over by a senior named Ralph Mason, who was the major of the school battalion.

"I am glad to meet you," said Major Mason, as he shook hands cordially. "I hope you will make yourselves at home," and he smiled in a manner that won the confidence of all the boys at once.

The meal was a good, substantial one—for Colonel Colby believed in setting a homelike table—and soon the clatter of knives and forks and the rattle of dishes filled the air. Most of the boys had come in from long journeys and were, consequently, hungry, so but little was said while the meal progressed. Spouter and Fatty and several other boys they had met sat at a table next to that occupied by the Rovers, but Nappy Martell and his cronies were on the opposite side of the mess hall, for which our friends were thankful.

"I think if I had to look at the face of Codfish while I was eating, it would spoil my appetite," was Andy's comment during the meal. "They ought to photograph his mouth and put it in the comic supplements."

"Yes. Or else they ought to get him to act in some of the funny movies," returned his twin.

As soon as the repast was at an end, Fred sought out Professor Brice and asked him if anything had been learned concerning the missing suitcase.

"I am sorry to say I haven't learned anything," answered the professor, a troubled look coming over his face. "I really must say, Rover, I don't know what to make of it. Do you suspect anyone in particular of having taken it?"

Fred was on the point of mentioning Nappy Martell's name, but suddenly held himself in check.

"I wouldn't like to say anything about that, Professor," he

Arthur M. Winfield

answered slowly. "I might be accusing a fellow cadet unfairly. If the suitcase isn't returned by to-morrow I may have something to say about it."

"Very well. I think I understand how you feel about it," and the young professor looked knowingly at the boy. "Did you have much in the suitcase?"

"Yes, sir. It was well packed. You see, I wasn't sure whether my trunk would come right along, so I carried all I could in my handbaggage."

When Fred joined the others, all of the crowd, led by Spouter, walked down to the gymnasium. Here the Rovers were introduced to a number of other pupils, including Ned Lowe, who was quite a mandolin player and also a good singer, and a tall, studious youth named Dan Soppinger.

"Ned is our great singer," announced Spouter. "We expect some day that he'll be singing in grand opera on the Metropolitan stage."

"Did you say grand opera or grand uproar?" questioned Andy, slyly.

"Opera, my boy! Opera!" repeated Spouter. "I expect some day that he will thrill great audiences with exquisite renderings of the famous solos by Wagner, Beethoven, Mozart, Donizetti—"

"Great mackerel, Spouter! what are you giving us—a musical directory?" interrupted Randy.

"No. I was only giving you a list of the things I expect to hear Ned sing sooner or later. Now, as for Dan here—he is the human encyclopedia."

"If there is anything you don't want to know, ask Dan and he'll be sure to tell you all about it," put in Fatty with a grin. "How about it, Dan?"

"Say! that's a fine way to introduce a fellow," cried Dan Soppinger, with a doubtful grin on his studious face. "Of course, I'm trying to learn as much as possible, but there are a whole lot of things that I don't know, and I'm not ashamed to acknowledge it. But say! by the way, can any of you tell me what the date was when Jefferson was inaugurated president?"

At this question there came a sudden groan, not only from Fatty, but also from Spouter and Ned Lowe. Then with one voice the three shouted:

"Down with him! He's at it again!"

"I don't believe any of you know the date," retorted Dan Soppinger. "If you did, you'd tell me. I am writing an article about the presidents, and I've got to put that in. And then, here's another thing. Can any of you tell me who crossed the Pacific Ocean to—"

But whatever the question was, it was never finished, for at that moment Spouter, Fatty, Ned and several others piled on Dan Soppinger and brought him to the gymnasium floor.

"Hi! You let up!" cried the victim, squirming from under the others as best he could. "Can't a fellow ask a question or two without you starting such a rough-house as this?"

"No questions to be asked, Dan, until the regular school term begins," answered Spouter. "Then all you've got to do is to go to the Rover boys—"

"Not much!" came simultaneously from Andy and Randy.

"Do you take us for a school library?" questioned Fred, gaily.

"I'll answer all the easy ones, Dan," said Jack, good-naturedly. "The hard ones I'll turn over to Spouter. If the question is a real sensible one, he'll give you a nice little answer—one about twelve hundred words long."

"Hurrah! Spouter is discovered at last!" cried Fatty. "Twelve hundred words long just fits it—that is, if Spouter is in a hurry to cut it short."

The Rover boys were much interested in what was taking place in the gymnasium, and they even tried out some of the bars and swinging rings, as well as one of the exercising machines.

"This is certainly an up-to-date institution," remarked Jack. "This gym couldn't be better."

"How about the boats?" questioned Randy. He and his brother had owned a rowboat on the Hudson River, and had often gone out in the craft.

"Oh, we've got half a dozen good rowboats, as well as several racing shells," answered Spouter. "You'll probably get a chance to look them over later."

While the Rover boys were taking in the sights to be seen in and around the gymnasium, their attention was attracted to a tall, well-formed cadet who was doing some clever work on one of the bars.

"He's doing that almost as well as a circus performer," was Fred's comment.

"Yes; he's certainly very graceful," returned Jack. "I wonder who he is."

"That is Walt Baxter," announced a cadet who had heard the talk.

"Walt Baxter!" exclaimed Randy. "I wonder if he can be the son of Dan Baxter, the man who made so much trouble for our fathers while at Putnam Hall."

"I'll soon find out," returned Jack. "But please remember— Dan Baxter reformed, and more than likely his son is a first-rate fellow."

As soon as Walter Baxter had gotten through with his exercise and had dropped to the floor, Jack, followed by his cousins, went up to him.

"Are you Walt Baxter—the son of Mr. Daniel Baxter?" he questioned.

"Yes," returned the other, and looked at Jack and the others with him curiously.

"I am Jack Rover—the son of Mr. Richard Rover. These are my cousins," and Jack introduced them.

"Oh! is that so?" answered Walt Baxter, and shook hands rather doubtfully. "I—I—am glad to know you," he stammered.

"And we are real glad to know you, Baxter," answered Randy, readily. "We heard you were at this school. We hope that we'll all be good friends."

"If we are not, it won't be my fault," and now there was a

Arthur M. Winfield

ring of relief in Walter Baxter's voice. He lowered his tone a trifle. "I know your fathers did a lot for my father, and I am very thankful for it. If I can do anything for you fellows here, I'll certainly do it."

"And we'll do what we can for you, Baxter," answered Jack, quickly.

After that the talk became general, and Walt Baxter told much about himself and the doings of the cadets at Colby Hall. When Nappy Martell's name was mentioned, he drew down the corners of his mouth.

"I never had any use for that chap," he declared. "Once or twice my hot temper got the better of me and we came pretty near having a fight. But after that Martell gave me a wide berth."

"I think I've got Martell to thank for something that is missing," said Fred, and thereupon related the particulars regarding the lost suitcase.

"Say! I think I know something about that!" cried Walter Baxter, quickly. "Yes, I'm sure I do!"

"Did you see Martell take the suitcase?" demanded the youngest Rover, quickly.

"I can't say as to that, exactly. But I did see Martell sneaking off through the backyard, past the stable, with something under his arm—a big package wrapped up in a couple of newspapers."

"When was this?" questioned Jack, quickly.

"About four o'clock this afternoon."

"Just after we arrived at the Hall!" burst out Randy.

"What did he do with what package?" asked Jack.

"I don't know exactly, excepting that he went down past the stable on to the roadway that leads to the farm fields."

"Maybe he took the suitcase and threw it down in one of the fields," ventured Andy.

"You didn't see him come back?" asked Fred.

"Yes, come to think of it, I did—about a quarter of an hour after that," answered Walt Baxter.

"And did he have the package then?"

"No."

"Then I'll wager it was the suitcase and he left it somewhere down on the farm!" cried Randy. "Let us go and take a look. We are permitted to go out in the farm fields, aren't we?" he asked of Walt.

"Oh, yes. You can go anywhere you please during off hours so long as you don't go out of bounds," was the reply. "If you want to go out of bounds, you have to report at the office and get permission."

The matter was talked over for a few minutes more, and Walt Baxter said he would gladly go along with the Rovers to show them just where he had seen Nappy Martell with the bundle. The five boys were soon in the neighborhood of the Hall stable, and then they passed beyond this to a roadway which ran between the fields attached to the school farm.

"It's a pity it's so dark," declared Jack. "I doubt if we'll be able to locate that suitcase even if we get quite close to it."

"I'll tell you what I'll do," declared Randy. "I'll run back to my room and get my pocket flashlight. That will be just the thing."

It took him but a few minutes to obtain the article he had mentioned, and with the flashlight to guide them, the five boys started along the roadway behind the school. The light was flashed first on one side and then on the other.

"Looks like a wild goose chase," declared Andy, after they had passed two farm fields. "I don't think he would come this far with that heavy suitcase."

"Here is a cornfield full of stacks," said Walt Baxter. "The stacks would afford a dandy hiding place for almost anything."

They approached the first of the stacks, and Fred kicked some of the corn stalks aside, but without result. Then they passed on to the next stack.

"Hello! here is something!" exclaimed Jack, as the rays of the flashlight fell upon the object. "Fred, I guess we've found it all right enough."

"So we have!" cried the youngest Rover; and in a moment more he thrust his hand in between the cornstalks and pulled out the missing suitcase.

CHAPTER XI

DOWN IN THE CORNFIELD

The other boys gathered around in curiosity as Fred brought forth from the stack of cornstalks his missing suitcase. Beside the bag were several newspapers crumpled up into a wad.

"Those must be the newspapers he had the suitcase wrapped in," remarked Walt Baxter.

"More than likely," answered Jack. He picked up the wad of papers and glanced at them. "New York newspapers, too," he cried. "Nappy must have brought them with him from home."

"Was the suitcase locked, Fred?" questioned Randy.

"No. I didn't bother to lock it, because, you see, I had it with me. I only lock a suitcase when I check it."

"Then you'd better take a look inside and see if your duds are all right," advised Andy.

The youngest Rover quickly unstrapped the suitcase and threw back the catch. Then, as Randy sent the rays of the flashlight into the bag, he, as well as the others, uttered various exclamations.

"The mean fellow!"

"Fred, you ought to get after him for this!"

For a quick look inside the suitcase had revealed the fact that Nappy Martell had opened the bag and thrown handfuls of dirt amid the pieces of clothing and the various other articles Fred had packed therein.

"You'll have to have all that laundered stuff done over again before you can wear it," declared Jack. "And you'll have to have those neckties cleaned, too, I am afraid. Say! this is a shame!"

"Just wait! I think I'll be able to get square with Nappy Martell," muttered the youngest Rover.

"He ought to be reported for this," broke in Walt Baxter. "This isn't a joke. It's a low-down, dirty trick."

At this remark all of the other Rover boys looked at Fred, and he looked at his cousins in return.

"I don't know about reporting this," he answered slowly. "I rather think I prefer to settle with Martell myself."

"That's the talk!" cried Andy. "If you reported this, some of the fellows might put you down for a softy and a sneak. I'd rather watch my chance and give Martell as good as he sent."

"And with interest," added his twin.

"If you fellows are anything like your fathers were before

you, I reckon you'll know how to get square with Nappy," remarked Walt Baxter. "I've heard that the Rovers never took a back seat for anybody."

"I'll figure out what I'm going to do after I get settled here," returned Fred. He suddenly began to smile. "Say! things have been happening since we left home, haven't they?"

"I should say yes!" answered Andy.

With Jack assisting his cousin in carrying the suitcase, the whole crowd returned to Colby Hall, and here the Rovers started to separate from Walt Baxter, first requesting him to remain silent regarding the finding of the handbaggage.

"If we don't say a word about it, maybe Nappy will get worried," said Fred; "and that is what I want him to do."

"He may go down to the cornfield to see if the bag is still there."

"Hold on!" burst out Randy, suddenly. "I've got an idea!" and then in a few words he explained what had occurred to him. The others listened with interest, and even Walt Baxter had to laugh outright over what he proposed.

"I'll do it!" declared the son of Dan Baxter, readily. "I'll do it the first chance I get. And, believe me, I'll fix it so Nappy Martell gets into hot water!"

"I'd like to see what effect the story has on Martell," said Andy, grinning broadly. "Can't you fix it so we can be around at the time?"

"Sure! When I get the chance, I'll drop you a hint."

Arthur M. Winfield

"And now I must get this bag to my room without anyone seeing me," said Fred.

"Better let Spouter or Fatty carry it up," advised Jack. "Then, if Martell sees it, he won't know that it is your suitcase."

It was an easy matter to get Spouter to do what was required, although he insisted upon knowing what was in the wind. When he was told, he, too, laughed heartily.

"It will serve Martell right," he said. "I hope it worries him to death."

As soon as the suitcase was safe in Fred's room, he sought out Professor Brice, who was busy arranging the order of some classes.

"I wish to report that I've got my suitcase back, Professor," said the youth.

"Ah, indeed!" was the teacher's reply, and his face showed his relief. "I'm glad to know it. Did you—er—have any trouble?"

"Nothing that I care to mention—at least at this time," answered Fred. "If you don't mind, Professor, we'll drop the matter."

"Oh, very well, Rover. Just as you please." The young professor looked at Fred rather knowingly. "Of course, if there is anything wrong, you can report it later," he added hesitatingly.

"Yes, sir. Thank you, sir," answered the youth, and then bowed himself out of the office. In the hallway he was joined by Andy.

"Did he make you squeal?" questioned the cousin quickly.

"Not much!" was the reply. "He's a good sport. I guess he's been through the mill himself."

Fred spent some time over the contents of the suitcase, brushing the dirt from some of the articles and sorting the rest out to be cleaned or laundered.

"It's going to cost two or three dollars to fix this up," he declared to Randy. "I really ought to send the bill to Martell."

"Well, just wait first and see if we get any fun out of this," answered the joke-loving cousin.

As was to be expected, there was far from a full night's sleep coming to the Rover boys that night. The quarters were strange to them, and there was more or less noise throughout the school building, a bunch of scholars coming in on a late train and not getting settled down until after midnight. There was also something of horseplay, although the majority of the cadets were too tired from their journeys to be very active.

"I suppose we'll have to stand some hazing and all that sort of thing later on," remarked Jack before retiring.

About one o'clock the school seemed to settle down, and then one after another the Rover boys fell asleep, not to awaken until the autumn sun was showing well above the hills beyond Clearwater Lake.

"This certainly is a splendid location," remarked Jack, as he went to the open window, stretched himself, and filled his lungs with the fresh morning air.

"I don't wonder Colonel Colby picked this place out for a school," answered Andy, who had come in. "He couldn't have done better."

Not being accustomed to their surroundings, it took the Rovers a little longer than usual to get washed and dressed. They were just finishing their toilets when there came a light knock on Randy's door. He opened it to find Walt Baxter standing there.

"Nappy Martell just went downstairs, and I've fixed that matter up with Ned Lowe," said Walt. "Come on down if you want to see what takes place."

He led the way, and all of the Rover boys followed at a safe distance. They saw Walt enter one of the big living-rooms of the Hall, to one end of which was attached the school library. Nappy Martell was at one of the library tables glancing carelessly over a magazine. In the living-room Walt was joined by Ned Lowe, and the pair walked up behind Nappy.

"Why, yes, it was the strangest thing I ever saw," said Walt to Ned in a loud voice so that Nappy Martell could not help but hear. "The fellow seemed to come from a stack of cornstalks down in the cornfield."

"It wasn't one of the cadets, was it?" questioned Ned, innocently.

"Oh, no. I think this fellow was some kind of a tramp— maybe some fellow who had been sleeping under the stack all night. But what he was doing with such a fine suitcase gets me."

"That's right. Tramps don't generally have suitcases," returned the other boy. "Did he come toward the school?"

"No. He dug out the other way just as fast as he could go."

"Poor fellow! maybe he was afraid if he came towards the school he would be arrested. If he had a suitcase he couldn't have been just an ordinary tramp. Maybe he was some working man looking for a job and without the price of a night's lodging."

"Perhaps, Ned. At the same time, I don't think Colonel Colby wants his cornstalks used for a hotel," returned Walt; and then he and Ned walked through the library and went outside on the campus.

During this conversation the Rover boys, hidden behind some open doors, had watched Nappy Martell closely. They had seen that he had caught what was being said and had immediately lost all interest in the magazine he was perusing. His face took on a worried look, and he glanced inquiringly after Walt and Ned. Then he threw down his magazine and started to leave the room.

"Come on, let us watch him," whispered Jack.

"Yes. But keep out of his sight," returned Randy. "We don't want this joke spoiled."

Keeping well in the background, they saw Nappy Martell ascend the stairs to his room. A moment later he came forth with his hat in his hand.

"I bet an oyster against a soda cracker he's going down to that cornfield!" cried Andy.

"Right you are!" answered Fred. "Come on, let's follow him;" and rushing up to their own rooms the Rover boys donned their caps and sweaters, for the day was unusually cool.

Nappy Martell left the Hall by a rear door, and the Rovers followed. They saw the loudly dressed youth hurry toward the stable and then disappear to the rear. Soon he was on the highway leading to the cornfield.

"There is no use of our following him, for he might see us and that would spoil everything," said Randy. "Let's wait here at the stable until he comes back."

It did not take Nappy Martell long to reach the cornfield; and from a distance the Rovers saw him rush around, first to one stack of cornstalks and then to another. He was gone fully a quarter of an hour, and came back looking decidedly worried.

"He thinks some tramp got that suitcase and went off with it," said Fred, grinning. "Randy, that certainly was one great joke."

"Don't say a word," answered Randy. "Just let him keep on worrying for a while. Maybe it will do him good."

As Martell passed the stable, the Rover boys stepped out of sight in the building. They saw him re-enter the Hall, and then they took a roundabout course which soon brought them to the campus, where they joined Fatty and Ned.

"It's certainly a good joke," was Fatty's comment. "And any fellow who would be mean enough to dirty a fellow's clothing like that ought to suffer for it. Gee! I'll bet he's worried!"

Of course, such a joke could not be kept entirely secret, and before long it was spread among a good many of the cadets. But great care was taken to keep it from Slugger Brown, Codfish and all the others belonging to the Martell crowd.

"And now to pay Martell back for his meanness!" said Fred a little later. "This joke of Randy's is all right as far as it goes, but I think I'm going to go him one better—that is, if I can get into Martell's room."

"All right, Fred. Anything you say goes," added Andy, quickly. "Isn't that so, Randy?"

"Sure thing!"

"Look here! You don't want to get into trouble," warned Jack.

"There won't be much trouble about this," answered Fred. "I am only going to give Nappy Martell something to think about."

Arthur M. Winfield

CHAPTER XII

LEARNING TO DRILL

While the Rover boys were talking matters over among themselves, Nappy Martell had returned to his room, which was connected by a door with that occupied by Slugger Brown.

"What in thunder made you run off in such a hurry, Nappy?" demanded the other cadet somewhat surlily. "You didn't answer that question I put to you at all."

"I had something else to think about," was the reply. "It looks to me as if I'm in hot water."

"How's that?"

"Do you remember I told you that I placed that Fred Rover's suitcase down under a stack in the cornfield?"

"Yes."

"Well, I heard Walt Baxter telling Ned Lowe that he had seen a tramp down in the cornfield running away from one of the stacks with a suitcase in his hand; so I went down to the cornfield to find out if the suitcase was still where I had hidden it. It was gone."

"Whew!" Slugger Brown gave a prolonged whistle. "That certainly does look bad. Did Baxter say where the tramp went?"

"He told Lowe that he had not come towards the Hall, but had gone off in the opposite direction."

"Then that looks as if the suitcase was gone for good."

"So it does. And I don't know what I'm going to do about it," answered Nappy Martell, gloomily. "Of course, I didn't think the suitcase would be stolen."

"And the worst part of it is, the Rovers suspect you of having taken it," was the comment of Slugger.

"Yes. But they can't prove it," cried Nappy, quickly. "That is, they won't be able to do it unless you or Codfish give me away."

"You know me well enough to know I won't say a word, Nappy. And as for Codfish, just give him to understand if he opens his trap you'll fix him for it."

A little while later Martell and Brown went below. In the lower hallway they met Fred and some of the others.

"Well, Martell, when are you going to return that suitcase?" demanded the youngest Rover.

"I told you I haven't got your suitcase and don't know anything about it," cried the loudly dressed youth. But at the same time his face grew flushed and he could not look Fred in the eyes.

Arthur M. Winfield

"You took that suitcase, and if you don't return it pretty quick you'll see what will happen," warned Fred; and then he walked away with his cousins, leaving Nappy Martell gazing at Slugger Brown, questioningly. The pair conversed in a low tone, and passed on out of the hall on to the campus.

"Now's your time, Fred, if you're going to do as you said," whispered Randy.

"Right you are!" was the quick reply. "Come on;" and Fred led the way upstairs again, his cousins following.

When they reached Nappy Martell's room, they found the door locked. But the door to Slugger Brown's apartment was unfastened, and they quickly entered this and passed into the room beyond.

"Say, Jack, won't you stand on guard?" questioned Fred. "They might come back while we're at work."

"All right, boys. But be careful what you do. You don't want to spoil anything. A joke is a joke, but it loses its flavor if it is carried too far."

With Jack standing in the hallway on guard, Fred and the twins took possession of Nappy Martell's room. The boy who loved to dress so loudly was rather methodical in his habits, and had arranged all of his clothing and other articles with great nicety in his chiffonier and his closet.

"The bed first," whispered Fred; and in a trice the boys had taken off the bed clothing and turned up the mattress. On the springs they placed one of the bedsheets and on the top of this they distributed all of Nappy's choice neckties and also his fancy-colored socks. Then to this they added his cuffs, his fancy underwear, and all of his loose jewelry. The articles were spread over the bed with care, so that they rested as flat as possible.

"Now, we'll put the mattress back and then make up the bed as nicely as possible," said Randy, who, of course, in a joke of this sort directed operations.

"Gee! I don't believe he'll find those articles in a hurry," chuckled Fred.

"They'll never find them until they come to turn the mattress over," vouchsafed Andy. "Some joke, believe me!"

"I was thinking about that clothing in the closet. I wonder if we can't fix that up some way," mused Randy. Then he began to grin. "Just the thing!" he continued, and walked to the chiffonier, from a drawer in which he brought out a package of safety pins.

"What are you going to do with those?" questioned Fred.

"We'll pin up all the ends of the sleeves and the trouser legs, from the inside," was the quick reply. "Come, hurry up!" and then the three boys lost no time in doing as Randy had suggested. This done, they left the room, leaving it, so far as looks in general went, just as when they had entered it.

"There'll be some fun when Nappy wants one of those neckties or a pair of those fancy socks," laughed Andy. "I wish I could be on hand to see him."

"Don't you worry—we'll hear about it," returned Fred. "He'll suspect me on account of that suitcase affair."

While it was true that the regular school term had not yet opened, the new arrivals had been informed that they must

Arthur M. Winfield

be on hand to be measured for their uniforms and also to be instructed by some of the seniors who were present in drilling. The measurements of the boys were taken down in the gymnasium under the directions of Mr. Silas Crews, who was the gymnasium instructor and also the husband of Mrs. Crews, the matron for the younger cadets.

"I hope they've got a suit on hand that fits me," was Jack's comment, as he and his cousins walked to the gymnasium. "I'd like to see how it feels to be in a uniform."

His wish was gratified, for a little later he was given an entire outfit, which consisted of both a fulldress uniform and a fatigue suit, as well as belt, shoulder straps, cap, and hat, and several other things. Uniforms were also found for the others, and the entire crowd lost no time in hurrying back to their rooms to dress up. In this they were aided by Spouter, who had donned his uniform immediately upon his arrival.

"Some brass buttons, believe me!" was Andy's comment, as he strode around the rooms.

"Say! you put me in mind of a peacock," said the twin. "My, just see how he swells up!" and Randy himself raised his chest as high as possible.

"What are you going to be, Jack—fifth corporal or first admiral of the rear guard?" questioned Fred.

"I'm going to be head soup-carrier for the bayonet squad," returned his cousin gaily.

As soon as they had donned their uniforms, the boys returned to the gymnasium, where they were placed in what was called an awkward squad, and which was under the direction of Dan Soppinger. Here they quickly learned how to stand erect with their toes on a chalk mark, and how to hold their hands properly. Then they were given directions how to cast their eyes "To the right," "To the left," and "Front." Then they learned the meaning of "Right face," "Left face," and "About face."

"All of you are doing pretty well," remarked Dan Soppinger to the squad of eight under him. "Now then, we'll see what you can do when it comes to marching. When I give the order 'Forward,' you balance on your right foot, and when the word comes 'March!' you step out with your left foot. And when you step out, do it like this," and he gave an illustration by marching up and down in front of the squad.

To the Rover boys all this was very interesting, and they learned with comparative ease. Only one of the awkward squad seemed to have difficulty in marching just right, a lad named White.

"Don't lag behind, White!" cried Dan Soppinger, sharply. "Step right out as if you meant it;" and after that White did a little better.

While the drilling was in progress, Colonel Colby came down to the gymnasium to look on. He was pleased with the general results.

"I think you are doing very well, boys," he said. "Of course, you can't learn to become first-class soldiers in a day. It takes hard practising to do anything just right."

"When do we get guns?" questioned Andy, after the drilling had come to an end.

"You won't get guns until you have learned how to march and how to turn properly," answered Dan. "Then, when you do get guns, you'll have to go in for the manual of arms."

"And how about learning how to shoot?" questioned Jack.

"That will come still later—after you have had experience in marching and in handling your guns."

"Whoop! Me for a real soldier boy!" cried Andy, his eyes sparkling, and then he began to hum a bit of doggerel he had made up on the spur of the moment.

"Johnny, get your musket—
You must get your musket.
Johnny, get your musket—
You must get it now!"

"Wow! that's some song," was Fred's comment. "Better have it copyrighted, Andy."

"Oh, I've already got a double-barreled patent on it," was the light answer. "Anybody who steals it will get ten years in a bathing suit at the north pole;" and at this there was a general laugh.

The boys were awaiting the arrival of Gif Garrison, who came in about noon of that day. Gif was a big boy, and, as mentioned before, was at the head of a great many of the athletic doings of the school.

"Glad to see you fellows here," said Gif, as he shook hands all around. "My! but we're going to have some good times now, aren't we?"

"If we don't, it won't be our fault," responded Jack.

"We've just been learning how to become soldiers,"

explained Randy. "My head is full of 'Eyes right,' 'Left face,' 'Forward march,' and all that sort of thing."

"Oh, you'll get used to that, Randy, before you've been here very long," returned Gif.

"Did you have a nice time getting here?" questioned Fred.

"I might have had a nice time if it hadn't been for one thing," was the answer. "I came in on the same train with a professor that none of us like."

"Oh! Do you mean Asa Lemm?" questioned Andy, quickly.

"That's it! What do you know of him?"

"We know quite a little," answered Jack, and related some of the particulars of what had happened on the train.

"Oh, I can see your finish," said Gif with a serious look on his face. "Old Lemon will never forget that happening. He'll be down on you for it all the term."

Arthur M. Winfield

CHAPTER XIII

FRED IS FOLLOWED

It took the Rover boys several days to settle down at Colby Hall. Everything, of course, was new to them, and they took great delight in roaming around the place in company with Spouter, Gif and the various new friends they had made. During that time they continued to drill, both in the morning and the afternoon; and it was surprising how quickly they learned the manual of arms and also the other tactics which go to make up the discipline of a cadet.

"This life is all to the merry," was Andy's comment one day, while he and the others were down at the shore of the river inspecting the boathouse with its numerous craft.

"It certainly is one fine place," answered Jack. "If Putnam Hall was anything like this, no wonder our fathers thought so much of it."

Since Fred had asked Nappy Martell for the suitcase, the boy who was addicted to loud clothing had avoided the Rovers. But through the cadet named White they had learned much of what had happened in Nappy's room when he came in after it had been "rearranged" by the Rovers.

"Nappy Martell was the maddest fellow you ever saw," Bart White had declared. "He stormed all around the corridor, accusing nearly everybody in that vicinity of having taken his neckties and his underwear and a lot of jewelry. He even came to my room and threatened to tell Colonel Colby if I didn't tell him where the things were."

"And, of course, you couldn't do that," had been Randy's reply, with a side wink at the others.

"No. I told him I didn't know where the things were—because, you see, I really didn't know," went on Bart White, innocently.

"And after that?" queried Jack.

"Oh, he stormed around, accusing this one and that one until some of the boys got sick of listening and told him to shut up. Then he went back to his room and slammed the door hard enough to burst it off its hinges."

"Do you suppose he reported the matter to Colonel Colby?" had been Fred's question.

"I don't know about that. You see, when a fellow gets as mad as Martell was he's liable to do almost anything." And that was all Bart White had had to relate concerning the affair.

So far, the Rover boys had not had anything to do with Asa Lemm. They had met the sharp-faced professor once in the hallway and he had stared at them in a fashion which made Andy shiver.

"He's got it in for me all right!" had been the declaration of the fun-loving youth.

Arthur M. Winfield

"I guess Gif was right," had been Jack's comment. "He'll have it in for us the whole term. Too bad! I'd rather be friendly with every one than have any enemies."

The Rover boys were just leaving the boathouse after having admired the beautiful four-and eight-oared shells stored there, when they saw Fatty Hendry coming towards them as rapidly as his stoutness permitted.

"Say! I've got something to tell you fellows," puffed the fat boy as he came closer. "I just saw that sneak of a Codfish coming from Fred's room. He looked awful sneakish, and I'm sure he was up to no good."

"I'll go up to my room at once and see," answered the youngest Rover, and lost no time in speeding back to the Hall.

He bounded up the stairs two steps at a time. But when he reached the room he occupied, a surprise awaited him. Everything was exactly as he had left it. It may be as well to state here that every cadet at Colby Hall was required to keep his room in absolute order, and a monitor came around twice a day to see that this regulation was carried out. If a pupil was lax in any particular regarding his room, he was given a demerit in consequence thereof.

"Well, thank goodness! he didn't upset anything, even if he was here," murmured Fred to himself. "I wonder what the little imp was up to?" Then a sudden thought struck him and he walked to the clothes closet in the bottom of which he had deposited his suitcase. He found the bag in the closet, but it was placed there in such a way that he was sure it had been handled.

"Well, what have you found?" questioned Andy, who had

followed his cousin to the room.

"I think I know why he came here," declared Fred. "More than likely Martell sent him here to find out whether I really had the suitcase or not. The bag I know has been handled. When I placed it in the closet I put the open end of the straps against the wall. Now the open ends are on this side."

"Say! you're some detective, Fred!"

"I know how I left the bag. And he certainly had it out of the closet and put it back."

"See if he did anything to it," went on Andy, quickly; and thereupon Fred brought the bag forth and examined it. It was empty, just as he had left it.

"Well, that will take the worry of the missing bag from Martell's mind," was Fred's comment, as he and Andy left the room, this time locking the door.

"Martell must have had some kind of a clue to the truth or he wouldn't have sent Codfish here," was Andy's comment. "Maybe he got on to what part Walt Baxter and Ned Lowe played in the trick." And in this surmise Andy was correct. By the merest accident Codfish had overheard Walt and Ned speaking about the joke, and at once he had gone to Nappy with the news; and the upshot had been that Nappy had sent the sneak to Fred's room to learn if the suitcase with Fred's initials upon it was there.

Late that afternoon both the old and the new cadets were assigned to their places in the various classrooms and also given the text-books which they were to study during the term.

Arthur M. Winfield

"This begins to look like work," sighed Randy.

"Well, we didn't come here just for the fun of it," declared Jack. "We came here, if you'll remember, to get an education."

"Oh, I'm not going to complain," returned his cousin quickly. "I'm willing to do my share of studying. But after the splendid vacation we had this Summer it will be a little tough at the beginning to get down to the grind."

"That's just what I was thinking," declared Andy. "I wish a fellow didn't have to study. Why can't some of our great inventors invent some kind of knowledge pill so a fellow can just go and buy a few boxes and then take them regularly?"

"Great idea, Andy!" exclaimed his twin merrily.

By the next morning all of the cadets had arrived, and also all of the teachers and the other persons connected with Colby Hall. Then the cadets were assembled on the parade ground and made to march into the general assembly room of the institution, where Colonel Colby addressed them. He spoke about the good work done by the cadets during the former term at the school, and said he trusted that the present term would turn out still better.

"At present all of our old officers of the battalion will hold over," he announced. "But in the near future—just as soon as we have got settled in our classes—I will announce the time for a new election. The major and the two captains to be elected must be in their senior year at this institution. The other officers may be either sophomores or juniors."

"That lets us out," whispered Andy to Jack. "Evidently no freshmen can be officers."

"Well, why should we be officers?" answered his cousin. "We hardly know a thing about soldiering yet. I think Colonel Colby's rule is a very good one."

During the meeting in the assembly room all of the professors were called on to say a few words to the cadets. The addresses delivered by Professors Grawson and Brice and one or two of the other teachers were well received; but it was plainly evident that when Asa Lemm came forward to speak to the boys there was a distinctly cold feeling towards him.

"I want to speak about attention to work," he said in a severe tone of voice. "During the last term at this school there was not that attention in classes that I desire. From now on I expect every one who comes to me to pay strict attention at all times. Any laxity will be severely punished."

"Gosh! He's a cheerful customer!" was Fred's comment.

"He'd make a fellow down on him almost before the term began," was another cadet's comment.

"I don't wonder they call him old Lemon," added another youth.

"And now we're all ready to go to work," said Jack, after the cadets had been dismissed. On the following day the classes were to begin.

There had been so much bustle and confusion throughout the school that day that Fred, who was not feeling extra well, got quite a headache.

"You had better lie down for a while and rest," said Jack, kindly. "You don't want to get sick."

"Oh, it's only a headache, and I'll soon be over it," declared Fred. "I think I'll go out for a quiet walk along the river."

"Do you want me to go along?"

"No. I'd just as lief go alone, Jack. I think the quietness will do me more good than anything."

This mood was not a new one with the youngest Rover, so Jack said no more, and a few minutes later Fred slipped on his heavy sweater and donned his cap and set out for his walk. His steps took him towards the boathouse and the bathing houses, and then he continued on along a path running close to the shore of the river.

Although the youngest Rover did not know it, his departure had been watched by Codfish. The small boy lost no time in hurrying to Nappy Martell and Slugger Brown with his information.

"You're sure he's alone?" asked Nappy, quickly.

"Yes. Nobody went out with him."

"Then that's our chance, Slugger," went on the boy from New York. "Come ahead, if you want to help me."

"All right, Nap. But I thought you said you could polish him off alone?"

"So I can. But I thought you'd like to see the fun."

"Can't I go along too?" put in Codfish.

"Yes, if you'll promise to keep your mouth shut about it."

"Oh, I won't say a word," returned the little cadet, quickly.

Putting on their hats and coats, the three cadets lost no time in following Fred. It was quite dark on the campus and parade ground, but they soon caught sight of the figure ahead as the youngest Rover moved past the bathhouses to the river path beyond.

"He's alone all right enough," was Slugger Brown's comment.

"I thought I'd catch him sooner or later after I set Codfish to watching him," answered Nappy Martell. "Now I guess I'll be able to teach him to play tricks on me," he added sourly.

The three cadets quickened their pace, and in a moment more caught up to Fred just as he reached a point on the river shore almost out of sight of the Hall. Fred had dipped his handkerchief in the water and used the same for wiping off his aching brow.

"See here, Rover, I want to talk to you!" cried Nappy Martell, and, striding forward, he caught Fred roughly by the arm.

Of course, the youngest Rover was startled, not dreaming that anyone was following him. Yet he showed no signs of fear.

"What do you want of me, Martell?" he asked quietly.

"I'll show you what I want of you!" cried Nappy Martell in sudden wrath. "I'll teach you to play tricks on me! Try to make me believe your suitcase was stolen, will you? And then come to my room and rough-house things, eh? Just wait till I get through with you and you'll wish you'd never been born!"

Arthur M. Winfield

CHAPTER XIV

THE FIGHT

Fred Rover realized that he was in an unenviable situation. Nappy Martell was thoroughly angry, and evidently Slugger Brown and Codfish were present to aid him in anything he might undertake to do.

Many another boy might have thought discretion the better part of valor and taken to his heels. But the youngest Rover was not built that way. He had been taught to stick up for his rights and defend himself whenever the cause was a just one.

"What do you propose to do, Martell?" he questioned as quietly as he could.

"I'll show you what I'll do," blustered the other. "You thought it was a fine joke to put most of my things under the mattress of my bed, didn't you?"

"Who told you I did that?"

"Never mind. I found it out, and that's enough. Do you dare to deny it?"

"I don't suppose there will be any use in denying it," was

Fred's reply. "It was done as a joke, to square accounts over the missing suitcase."

"Bah! you needn't talk to me, Rover! I know the kind you and your cousins are. I'm going to fix you. How do you like that?" and as he uttered the last word, Nappy Martell hauled back and slapped Fred on the cheek.

It was a comparatively light blow, but it aroused all the fighting blood in the youngest Rover boy's nature, and without stopping to think twice, he doubled up his fists and hit the larger youth a stinging blow in the jaw.

"Gee! look at that!" murmured Codfish, who had not expected such an onslaught from the smaller cadet.

"Say, Nappy, he's coming back at you!" burst out Slugger Brown, in surprise.

"Coming back at me nothing!" roared Martell; and, leaping forward, he rained a succession of blows on Fred—hitting him in the shoulder, the chest and then the left ear.

In another moment the two cadets were at it "hammer and tongs." As they circled around, Codfish put out his foot, trying to trip Fred up. He failed in this, but a moment later Slugger Brown tried the trick with success, and the youngest Rover came down heavily and an instant later Nappy Martell landed on top of him.

"Get off of me! That wasn't fair!" exclaimed Fred. "Those other fellows tripped me up."

"Aw, shut up!" retorted Martell; and while he held Fred down with his body he continued to pommel the smaller youth with his fists.

"Don't go too far," said Slugger Brown presently, in alarm. "If you do that, he may squeal and get you into trouble."

"Somebody is coming!" screamed Codfish, suddenly, as he saw a number of forms running across the parade ground in the direction of the river road. "Four or five of 'em."

"It's Jack Rover and his chums," muttered Slugger Brown.

He was right. Jack was approaching, followed by Spouter, Fatty, Walt Baxter and Gif Garrison.

"I was sure they were up to no good—following Fred that way," Walt Baxter was saying.

"I'm glad you told me about this, Walt," answered Jack. "Three against one is no fair deal."

As the five cadets came rushing up, Codfish viewed their approach with alarm and then retreated several paces. Slugger Brown, however, stood his ground.

"Hi you! let my cousin alone!" cried Jack, and, leaping forward, he caught Nappy Martell by the collar and hurled him into some bushes.

"Say, this isn't any of your fight," put in Slugger Brown, uglily. While he spoke, Fred lost no time in leaping to his feet and there he stood, once more on the defensive.

"No one asked you to butt in, Jack Rover!" stormed Nappy Martell. "You keep out of this."

"Why did he attack you, Fred?"

"Huh! you know the reason as well as he does," burst out

Martell. "You played a trick on me about that suitcase, and then you came and rough-housed my room."

"One trick was only played to square up for the other, Martell," answered Jack, calmly. "You ought to be man enough to cry quits and let it go at that."

"I won't cry quits—not until I've given this fellow a good licking!" roared Nappy Martell; and then before anyone could stop him he lunged another blow at Fred, who, however, was quick enough to dodge it.

"Stop!" Jack's voice was now unusually stern, and stepping up to Nappy Martell he caught the fellow by the arm and swung him around so that the pair faced each other. "If you want to fight, Martell, take somebody nearer your size."

"Oh, Jack! I'm not afraid of him," burst out Fred. Strange to say, the excitement of the occasion seemed to have chased his headache completely away.

"Maybe you want me to fight you," sneered Nappy Martell.

"You'll have to fight me if you don't leave my cousin Fred alone."

"See here, Rover! you've no right to butt in like this," interposed Slugger Brown. "Why don't you let the pair finish it?"

"Those two fellows," cried Fred, pointing to Slugger Brown and Codfish, "tripped me up. It wasn't fair—three against one."

"We didn't trip him up at all," came from the two accused ones simultaneously.

Arthur M. Winfield

"They did, Jack. First Codfish tried it, and then Brown put out his foot and I went down, and Martell at once pounced on me."

"That's no way to fight!" broke out Spouter.

"It was certainly a mean trick," was Gif's comment.

"If there is any fighting to be done, I guess we're on hand to see that it's done fairly," came from Walt Baxter.

A perfect war of words followed, in the midst of which Nappy Martell seemed to lose complete control of his temper. He rushed at Jack and hit the youth two quick blows, one in the chest and the other on the chin. The oldest Rover was not looking for this attack, and he staggered backward into some bushes, all but losing his balance.

"That's the way to do it, Nappy!" cried Slugger Brown, excitedly. "Give it to him!"

Jack was as much surprised as Fred had been when first hit, but he was able to recover much more quickly than his cousin. He leaped forward from the bushes, doubled up his fists, and the next instant sent in a crashing blow that landed straight on Martell's nose. He followed up this blow with another on the other youth's chin which sent Martell sprawling flat on his back.

"Hurrah! that's the way to do it, Jack!" cried Spouter.

"Say! has he got to fight two of you Rovers?" questioned Slugger Brown.

"No. He's got to fight me only," answered Jack, quickly. He turned to his cousin. "Fred, you keep out of this."

"But he started on me," pleaded the youngest Rover. "And now that you are here to see fair play, I'm not afraid of him."

"Never mind. It's my fight, anyway," went on Jack. "I owe him one for the way he treated me down in Wall Street that day."

While this talk was going on, Nappy Martell had scrambled to his feet. His nose was swollen and bleeding profusely.

"You imp!" he howled, and lunged another attack at Jack.

He was able to land two blows on Jack's chest, but they were not powerful enough to do harm. Then, as Martell circled around, the oldest Rover boy managed to get in another blow, this time on his opponent's mouth, loosening two of Nappy's teeth.

"That's the way to do it, Jack!"

"Give him a few more like that and he'll soon quit."

"Go for him, Nappy! You can do him up if you'll only try," bellowed Slugger Brown in excitement.

"You keep back, Slugger," warned Walt Baxter. "Don't you interfere."

"I didn't interfere."

"Well, you're too close, anyway. Keep back like the rest of us."

"That's just what I say," broke out Spouter.

Realizing that the others were in the majority, Slugger

Brown kept his distance from the pair who were fighting. Codfish was trembling like a leaf, and cowered well in the background.

Around and around circled the two contestants, and for a few minutes neither of them seemed to have the advantage. Jack was hit in the arm, and returned by landing another blow, this time on Nappy's chest. Then the big youth aimed a kick at the Rover boy's stomach.

"Hi! that's no way to fight!" cried Gif, indignantly.

Jack had managed to escape the kick, and he had put down one hand so quickly that Nappy Martell had been in great danger of being caught and thrown on his back.

In the midst of the contest several forms could be seen hurrying across the campus and the parade ground, and in a moment more Andy and Randy came into view, followed by Bart White and some other cadets.

"It's a fight!"

"Why, what do you know about this! Jack is fighting Nappy Martell!"

"Martell tackled me first, but Jack took the fight out of my hands," explained Fred to his cousins.

"Who has got the best of it?" questioned Bart White, excitedly.

"I think Jack has the best of it so far," answered Gif; "but the fight isn't finished yet," he added, a bit anxiously.

"You're right it isn't finished yet!" retorted Slugger Brown.

"Just you wait until Nappy gets his second wind, and then you'll see what he'll do to Rover."

Once more the two contestants were circling around, each trying to get in some kind of telling blow. Various passes were made, and in the excitement the pair left the roadway and began to circle around on the grassy bank of the river.

"Look out there, or you'll both go overboard!" sang out Spouter in alarm.

The cadets who were fighting were too engrossed to pay attention to this warning. They kept on circling about, and then Nappy Martell made a wild and vicious pass for Jack's head. The latter dodged like lightning, came up under his opponent's arm, and the next instant landed a swinging blow on Martell's ear which sent him staggering backward several paces, to fall with a splash into the river.

CHAPTER XV

IN THE TOWN

"Hello! Nappy's overboard!"

"Wow! that was some crack on the ear!"

"Can he swim?"

"Sure, he can swim! If he can't we can haul him in easy enough."

"I don't believe the river is very deep here."

Such were some of the words uttered immediately after the well-delivered blow from Jack Rover had sent his opponent spinning into the swiftly flowing waters of the Rick Rack River. Fortunately, the moon and the stars were shining brightly, so it was not as dark as it otherwise might have been. Indeed, had it not been for the brightness of the night it is doubtful if the fight could have been carried on as already described.

All of the cadets present lined up along the river bank, and an instant later saw Nappy Martell come to the surface. He was striking out wildly and spluttering at the same time, showing that he had gone overboard with his mouth open and had swallowed some of the water. One hand and shoulder were covered with mud from the river bottom, for at that particular point the stream was less than five feet deep.

"Oh, he'll be drowned! I know he'll be drowned!" screamed Codfish in terror.

"You shut up, you little imp!" burst out Gif. "You'll arouse the whole school, and there is no need of doing that."

By this time Nappy Martell was close to the river bank, and he reached up his hand appealingly to those above him.

"Here, give me your hand, Nappy!" cried Slugger Brown, and reached down to aid his crony. But the bank was a slippery and treacherous one, and he was in danger of going overboard himself.

"Wait a minute, Slugger—let me help you," cried Spouter, and he took hold of the big youth's left hand.

Then the others also came forward to do what they could, and in a few seconds more Nappy Martell was hauled up on the grass. He was pretty well exhausted and panted painfully.

"I'm sorry you went overboard, Martell," said Jack, promptly. "I didn't expect to knock you into the river."

"You did it on purpose! You know you did!" returned the other youth wrathfully. "Yo—you—d—d—don't know how to f—f—fight fair," he added, his teeth suddenly beginning to chatter, for the unexpected bath at this season had proved awfully cold.

"Say! he's shivering like a leaf!" cried Fred.

Arthur M. Winfield

"You had better get back to the Hall and change your clothing," advised Jack.

"I won't change anything until I've given you a licking," roared Nappy Martell.

"Oh, say, Nappy, you had better call it off for to-night," interposed Slugger Brown. "You can't fight in those wet clothes. Finish it some other time."

"I won't!" came the ejaculation, and then the dripping boy hurled himself once more at Jack.

But he was blinded by water and mud as well as by rage; and the oldest Rover boy easily evaded the new onslaught. Then, of a sudden, he reached out and caught Martell by both wrists and held him in a vise-like grasp.

"Now, see here, Martell, don't be foolish," he said sternly. "I don't want to fight a fellow who has been overboard and is wringing wet. You'll catch your death of cold hanging around here in this night air. Go on back to the Hall and change your clothing. If you want to finish this some other time, I'll be ready for you."

"That's the talk!" added Spouter.

"It would be foolish to go on in this condition," remarked Gif. "Call it off, by all means."

"You might as well do it," came from Slugger Brown. "You wouldn't have any kind of a fair show, Nappy—after having been in the river, and after having had to lick the other Rover first."

"He didn't lick me!" burst out Fred, indignantly.

More words followed, but in the end Nappy Martell consented to return to the Hall and went off in company with Slugger Brown, Codfish, and one or two more friends who had chanced to come up.

"You'll have to slip in on the sly, or else somebody may ask some unpleasant questions," remarked Slugger Brown on the way to the school.

"You lend me your coat, and I'll take mine off and make a bundle of it," answered Martell; and so it was arranged. The others clustered around the dripping youth and thus they managed to get him to his room without being detected.

"He'll never forgive you, Jack, for knocking him into the river," said Randy, while the Rovers and their friends walked slowly back to the Hall.

"I guess you're right," was the answer.

"And what is more, he'll probably try to play some under-handed trick on you," added Andy.

"I wish I had had the chance—I think I could have knocked him out myself," broke in Fred. "I'm not afraid of him, even if he is bigger than I am."

All those who had witnessed the contest were cautioned to keep quiet about it. Yet in a school like Colby Hall it was next to impossible to keep the particulars of the affair from circulating, and before long many of the cadets knew the truth. The majority were of the opinion that Jack could readily have defeated Martell had the contest been fought to a finish.

"He'll undoubtedly lay for you, Jack," remarked Fred that

night, in talking the matter over in their rooms.

"Maybe he'll lay for you, Fred," smiled his big cousin. "You had better keep your eyes peeled."

"I guess we had better all watch out," was Randy's comment.

But for the next few days Nappy Martell, as well as his particular crony, Slugger Brown, kept to themselves, while Codfish was so timid that he hardly dared to show himself.

About a week, including Sunday, went by, and the school began to settle down to its regular routine of studies. The Rover boys had had all their classes mapped out for them, and had also been assigned to a class in gymnasium work. Gymnastics especially suited the agile Andy, who nearly always preferred action to sitting still. The Rover boys on leaving home had promised their parents that they would pay strict attention to their studies, and now they did their best in that direction. Of course, some of the lessons were rather hard, and Fred, being the youngest, often found he needed assistance from the others.

During those days they quickly discovered why Dan Soppinger had been referred to by one of their friends as the "human question mark." Dan always wanted to know something, and he did not hesitate to ask for information on any and all occasions, no matter what else might happen to be under discussion at the time.

"He'll die asking questions," remarked Andy. "I never knew a fellow who could fire questions at a person so rapidly."

It was now ideal weather for football, and as soon as the school became settled football talk filled the air. Gif Garrison had been at the head of the football eleven the Fall previous, and now he was looked upon to whip the new team into shape.

"We generally play three games with outside schools," explained Gif to the Rovers one day. "First we play Hixley High. Then we play the Clearwater Country Club. And after that we wind up usually with our big game with Columbus Academy."

"It must be great sport," answered Jack.

"Did you ever get a chance to play football in New York?"

"Oh, yes, we occasionally played a game."

"Jack would make a first-rate football player if he had the chance," put in Randy. "I've seen him play, and I know."

"Yes. And Fred makes a pretty good player, too," added Andy. "Of course, he's small and light in weight, but he's as quick on his feet as they make 'em."

"How about you and Randy?" questioned Gif.

"Oh, we never cared very much to play football. We'd rather have some fun in the crowd looking on," was the answer of the twin.

At this, the football leader smiled. "Well, we've got to have some kind of an audience—otherwise there wouldn't be any fun in pulling off a game." He looked at Jack and Fred, thoughtfully. "I'm going to keep you two fellows in mind, and if I can put one or both of you on the team, I'll do it. Of course, you'll have your try-outs on the scrub first."

"Well, you can put me on the scrub as soon as you please,"

answered Jack, promptly.

"I'll be glad of the chance," added Fred.

As was to be expected, no sooner had the boys attempted to settle down at Colby Hall than they began to want for a number of things which they had failed to bring from home. These articles were, for the most part, of small consequence; yet the boys could not get along very well without them, and so resolved on the following Saturday, which was a holiday, to walk down to Haven Point and do some shopping.

"I'd like first rate to take a look around the town, too," said Randy. "It looked like a pretty good sort of place."

"Maybe we can go to the moving picture show there," put in his brother. "We'll have time enough."

"Perhaps—if the films look worth while," answered Jack.

They had already learned that the moving picture show in the town was of the better class, and that the pupils of the school were allowed to attend a performance whenever they had time to do so.

It did not take the four cousins long to walk the distance to Haven Point. They left the school directly after lunch, and inside of an hour had purchased the various small articles which they desired. Then all headed for the moving picture theater, which was located on the main street in the busiest portion of that thoroughfare.

As the boys walked up to the booth to purchase their admission tickets, they saw a bevy of girls just entering the door. They were all well dressed and chatting gaily.

"Nice bunch, all right," was Randy's comment. "I wonder where they are from?"

"I think I know," answered Jack. "Spouter was telling me there is a girls' school on the other side of this town, called Clearwater Hall. It's about as large as Colby Hall. More than likely those girls come from that school."

"I wish we knew them," said Andy. "I wonder if some of the cadets from our school don't know them."

"More than likely some of our fellows know some of the girls," said Jack. "We may be able to become acquainted with them some day."

Arthur M. Winfield

CHAPTER XVI

AT THE MOVING PICTURE THEATER

The moving picture theater was large enough to hold several hundred people, and when the boys entered they found the place almost full.

"There are some seats—over on the left," remarked Jack, as he pointed them out. "Two in one row and two directly behind."

"Why not two in one row and two directly in front?" returned Andy, gaily, and then headed for the seats.

"You and Fred had better sit in front, and Randy and I can take the back seats," went on Jack; and so it was arranged.

They had come in between pictures and while some doors had been open for ventilation, so that the place was fairly light. As Jack took his seat he noticed that the girls who had come in just ahead of the boys were sitting close by.

"They certainly do look like nice girls," was Jack's mental comment; and he could not help but cast a second glance at the girl sitting directly next to him. She was attired in a dark blue suit trimmed in fur and held a hat to match in her lap.

Jack noted that she was fair of complexion, with dark, wavy hair.

"I'm thinking this is going to be a pretty interesting picture for us, Andy," remarked Randy, as the name of the production was flashed upon the screen. "'The Gold Hunter's Secret—A Drama of the Yukon,'" he read. "That must have been taken in Alaska."

"That's right, Randy," returned his twin. "Gee! I hope this Alaskan play doesn't affect us; like that other Alaskan play once affected dad," he went on, referring to a most remarkable happening, the details of which were given in "The Rover Boys in Alaska."

"It isn't likely to," answered Randy, promptly. "Poor dad was in no mental condition to attend that show, Uncle Dick once told me. He had been knocked on the head with a footstool, and that had affected his mind."

The four Rovers were soon absorbed in the stirring drama of the Alaskan gold fields, and for the time being almost forgot their surroundings. In the midst of the last reel, however, Jack felt the girl beside him stirring.

"It's my hatpin," she whispered. "It just fell to the floor."

"I'll get it," he returned promptly, and started to hunt in the dark. He had to get up and push up his seat before the hatpin was recovered.

"Oh, thank you very much," said the girl sweetly, when he presented the article to her.

"You are welcome, I'm sure," returned the Rover boy; and then he added with a smile: "Accidents will happen in the best of families, you know," and at this both the girl and two of her companions giggled.

The photo-drama was presently finished and was followed by a mirth-provoking comedy at which the entire audience laughed heartily. Then came a reel of current events from various portions of the globe.

"Say, there's something worth looking at!" cried Fred, as a boat race was flashed on the screen.

"Right you are," responded Jack. "Just see those fellows pull! Isn't it grand?" he added enthusiastically. "I'd like to be in that shell myself," and he turned suddenly, to catch the girl beside him casting her eyes in his direction. She dropped them quickly, but her whole manner showed that she, too, was interested, not only in the race, but in what Jack had said. The cadets, of course, were in uniform, so the girl knew they were from Colby Hall.

The reel of current events had almost come to a finish, and there was intense silence as the picture showed the funeral of some well-known man of the East, when there came a sudden splutter from the operator's booth in the back gallery. This was followed by several flashes of light and then a small explosion.

"What's that?"

"Some explosion!"

"The theater's on fire!"

"Let's get out of this!"

"That's right! I don't want to be burnt to death!"

Such were some of the exclamations which arose on the air. A panic had seized the audience, and, like one person, they leaped to their feet and began to fight to get out of the theater. In a twinkling there was a crush in the aisles, and several people came close to being knocked down and trampled upon.

"Where's my hat?"

"Get back there—don't crush these children!"

"See the smoke pouring in!"

"Open the side door, somebody!"

"Keep cool! Keep cool!" yelled somebody from the gallery. "There is no fire! Keep cool!" But there was such a tumult below that scarcely anybody paid attention to these words.

While many fought to get out the way they had come in, others stormed towards the side doors of the playhouse. Meanwhile, an ill-smelling cloud of smoke drifted through the auditorium.

With the first alarm the Rover boys had leaped to their feet, and almost by instinct the others looked to Jack to see what he would do.

"Oh, oh! is the place on fire?" cried the girl who had been sitting next to the oldest Rover, and she caught him by the arm.

"I don't know," he answered. "Something exploded in the operating room."

"Oh, let us get out!" came from one of the other girls.

"Yes, yes! I don't want to be burnt up!" wailed a third.

"Don't get excited," warned Jack. "I don't believe there is any great danger. There is no fire down here, and there seem to be plenty of doors."

"The fellow upstairs said to keep cool," put in Randy. "Maybe it won't amount to much after all."

Most of the lights had gone out, leaving the theater in almost total darkness.

"Come on for the side door," said Jack. "That's the nearest way out."

The smoke from above was now settling, and this caused many to cough, while it made seeing more difficult than ever. Jack pushed Fred ahead of him, holding one hand on his cousin's shoulder, while with the other hand he reached out and grasped the wrist of the girl who had been sitting beside him.

"You had better come this way," he said; "and bring your friends along."

"All right. But do hurry!" she pleaded. "I am so afraid that something will happen."

"Oh, Ruth! can we get out?" questioned the girl next to her.

"I don't know. I hope so," answered the girl addressed, and then began to cough slightly, for the smoke was steadily growing thicker.

It was no easy matter to reach the side entrance, for already half a hundred people were striving to get through a doorway not much over two feet wide. The air was filled with screams and exclamations of protest, and for the time being in the theater it was as if bedlam had broken loose.

"Are we all here?" came from Andy, as, with smarting eyes, he tried to pierce the gloom.

"I'm here," answered his twin.

"So am I," came simultaneously from Jack and Fred.

Then Jack turned to the girl who was now beside him.

"Are all your friends with you?"

"I—I think so," she faltered; and then she added: "Annie, are Alice and Jennie with you?"

"Yes. We're all here," came from somebody in the rear. "But, oh, do let us get out! I can scarcely breathe!"

"I've lost my hat!" wailed another.

"Oh, never mind your hat, Alice, as long as we get out," came from the girl who was next to Jack.

At last the crowd at the doorway thinned out, and a moment later the four Rovers, pushing the girls ahead of them, managed to get outside. They found themselves in a narrow alleyway, and from this hurried to the street beyond.

"Oh, how glad I am that we are out of there!" exclaimed the girl who had been sitting beside Jack.

"I'm glad myself," he added, wiping away the tears which the smoke had started from his eyes.

"If only they all get out safely!" said one of the other girls.

"I don't know about that," answered Randy, seriously. "It was a bad enough crush at that side door, but I think it was worse at the front doors."

By this time everybody seemed to be out of the theater. An alarm of fire had been sounded, and now a local chemical engine, followed by a hook and ladder company, came rushing to the scene. There was, for fully ten minutes, a good deal of excitement, but this presently died down when it was learned positively that there was no fire outside the metallic booth from which the pictures had been shown and where the small explosion had occurred.

"It wasn't much of an explosion," explained the manager of the theater. "It was more smoke than anything else."

"Yes. And I yelled to the crowd that there was no fire and that they must keep cool," added the man who had been operating the moving picture machine.

In the excitement several people had been knocked down, but fortunately nobody had been hurt. A number of articles of wearing apparel had been left in the theater.

"I wish I could get my hat," said the girl named Alice, wistfully. "I don't want to go back to school bareheaded."

"What kind of a hat was it?" questioned Randy, who stood beside her. "Maybe I can get it for you;" and then, after the girl had given him a description of the head covering, he went off to question one of the theater men about it. In a few minutes more he came back with the missing property.

After Randy returned, the boys introduced themselves to the

girls, and learned that all of the latter were scholars at Clearwater Hall. The leader of the party was Ruth Stevenson, who had sat next to Jack, while her friends were Annie Larkins, Alice Strobell, Jennie Mason and May Powell.

"I know a fellow named Powell quite well," remarked Jack, as the last-named girl was introduced. "He goes to our school. His name is Dick, but we all call him Spouter."

"Dick Powell is my cousin," answered May. And then she added smilingly: "I've heard of you Rover boys before."

"Yes, and I've heard of you, too," broke in Ruth Stevenson.

"And who told you about us?" questioned Jack.

"Why, a big boy at your school—the head of the football team."

"Oh! do you know Gif Garrison?"

"Yes. I suppose you know him quite well?"

"Well, I should say so!" declared Jack. "Why, my cousin Fred here is named after Gif Garrison's father. His father and my father were school chums."

"Oh! Why then we know a lot of the same people, don't we? How nice!" returned Ruth Stevenson, and smiled frankly at Jack.

After that the talk between the boys and the girls became general, and each crowd told the other of how matters were going at their own particular school.

"Yes, I've been up to Colby Hall several times to see the

Arthur M. Winfield

baseball and the football games," said Ruth to Jack in answer to his question. "It's certainly a splendid place."

"Some day, if you don't mind, I'll come over and take a look at Clearwater Hall," he answered.

"Clearwater Hall! Say, that must be a fine place to get a drink!" piped in Andy; and at this little joke all of the girls giggled.

CHAPTER XVII

THE GIRLS FROM CLEARWATER HALL

The Rover boys remained with the girls from Clearwater Hall for the best part of half an hour after the scare at the moving picture theater, and during that time the young folks became quite well acquainted.

"We'll have to be getting back to our school now," said Ruth Stevenson, presently.

"Oh, what's your hurry?" pleaded Jack. "Weren't you going to stay to the pictures?"

"No. We were going to leave immediately after that reel they were showing when the explosion occurred," the girl replied.

"Well, we've got to get back to Colby Hall in time for supper; but we can make that easily enough—we are all good walkers."

"I should think you would ride in your auto-stage," put in Alice Strobell. "I'd ride if we had a stage handy."

"The stage isn't down here now," answered Randy. "It only comes on order."

The four boys walked with the girls to the end of a side street of the town, and there the pupils from Clearwater Hall stopped to say good-bye.

"We are very thankful for what you did for us at the theater," said Ruth Stevenson. "You were very kind, indeed."

"You are regular heroes!" burst out May Powell, who by her merry eyes showed that she was almost as full of fun as were the Rover twins. "I'm going to write to Spouter and let him know all about it."

"And don't forget to mention the rescue of my hat," added Alice Strobell with a giggle.

"I hope I have the pleasure of meeting you again, Miss Stevenson," said Jack, in an aside to the oldest girl of the party.

"Well, maybe," she returned, looking at him frankly.

"I've enjoyed this afternoon very much—in spite of that excitement."

"Oh, so have I!" and now she cast down her eyes while a faint flush stole into her cheeks.

"We won't dare say much about that trouble in the theater when we get back to school," remarked Jennie Mason.

"That's right!" burst out Annie Larkins. "If we did, maybe Miss Garwood would refuse to let us attend any more performances."

"Is Miss Garwood the head of your school?" questioned Randy.

"Yes. And let me tell you, she is a very particular and precise woman."

"I guess she isn't as precise and particular as one of our professors," was Andy's comment.

"Oh! do you mean that teacher they call old Lemon?" cried May Powell.

"Yes."

"We've met him a number of times. What a ridiculous man he is! I don't understand why Colonel Colby keeps him."

"I saw you look at me when I spoke about that boat race," said Jack to Ruth Stevenson. "Maybe you like to be out on the water?"

"Oh, I do—very much! You know we have boats at the school, and I often go out with my friends."

"I like to row myself. Perhaps some day you'd like to go out with me?" went on the oldest Rover, boldly.

"I'd have to ask permission first," answered the girl, and then dropped her eyes. Evidently, however, the tentative invitation pleased her.

As was to be expected, the parting between the boys and the girls was a rather prolonged affair, and it looked as if everybody was highly pleased with everybody else. But at last Annie Larkins looked at a wrist watch she wore and gave a little shriek.

"Oh, girls, we must be going! We ought to be at the school this minute!"

Arthur M. Winfield

"Then here is where we start the walking act," declared May Powell. "Good-bye, everybody!" and away she hurried, leaving the others to trail behind her.

"Don't forget about the row," said Jack in a low tone to Ruth Stevenson.

"I'll remember—if I get the chance," she returned; and in a moment more all of the girls were gone and the boys retraced their steps to the center of the town.

"Pretty nice bunch," was Randy's comment.

"It's funny that Spouter Powell never told us he had such a nice cousin," came from Fred.

"Hello, Fred's already smitten!" cried Jack, gaily.

"Huh! you needn't talk," retorted the youngest Rover. "How about yourself? Didn't I catch you trying to make a date with that Ruth Stevenson?"

"Oh, say, Fred! your ears are too big for your head," retorted Jack, growing red, while Andy and Randy looked at each other suggestively.

By this time the excitement around the moving picture theater had died away completely and the crowd had disappeared. The front doors were closed, but the manager was just hanging out a sign to the effect that the evening performances would be given as usual.

"I guess it was a big scare for nothing," was Randy's comment.

"The audience can be thankful that they got out without

anybody being hurt," returned Jack.

The boys made a few more purchases in Haven Point, and then started back for Colby Hall.

"I wonder if those girls go to church in Haven Point on Sundays," remarked Jack, just before the Hall was reached.

"I don't know," answered Andy. "More than likely." His eyes began to twinkle. "Thinking of going to church yourself, Jack?"

"Didn't we go to church when we were at home, Andy?"

"Sure," was the prompt reply.

"I think we can find out from Spouter or from some of the other cadets," answered Fred. "I know the boys are allowed to go to whatever church they please on Sundays." It may be as well to add here that on week days regular chapel exercises were held at Colby Hall before the ordinary classes were in session.

From Spouter Jack received the information he desired, which was to the effect that his cousin May and a number of her chums generally attended a church on the outskirts of Haven Point in the direction of Clearwater Hall.

"If you say so, I'll go with you there to-morrow morning," continued Spouter; and so the matter was arranged. At the church the cadets heard a very good sermon, and after the services had the pleasure of strolling with the girls as far as the entrance to their school grounds.

Monday morning found the Rovers once more down to the grind of lessons. So far they had gotten along very well. But on Tuesday the unfortunate Andy had another run-in with Asa Lemm.

"This won't do at all, Rover," stormed the professor, after Andy had given the wrong answer to a question. "You must pay more attention to your studies."

"I'm doing the best I can, Professor," pleaded the youth.

"Nonsense! I don't believe a word of it. They tell me you spend most of your time in horseplay. Now, that won't do at all. You must buckle down to your studies or I shall have to take you in hand;" and Professor Lemm glared at the lad as if ready to devour him.

"Say, Andy, you'll have to toe the chalk mark after this," whispered his twin. "If you—"

"Silence there! I will have silence!" cried Asa Lemm, pounding on his desk with a paper weight.

"I'll have one grand smash-up with that man some day," was Andy's comment in speaking of the affair after the school session had closed. "I can't stand his arbitrary ways."

"Oh, he's a lemon—and worse," returned his brother.

During that week there was an election of officers for the school battalion, composed of Company A and Company B. The Rover boys, being freshmen, could not compete for any position, even had they so desired; but there was a good deal of electioneering among the cadets, and the lads got quite a lot of fun out of it. The announcement of who was elected was followed by a parade around the grounds and an unusually good supper in the mess hall. Then the boys were allowed to gather at one end of the parade ground near the river, where they soon had several large bonfires burning, around which they danced, sang, and cut up to their hearts' content.

The election had been a bitter disappointment to Slugger Brown and Nappy Martell. Each had wanted to be an officer of the battalion, and each had failed to get the required number of votes.

"It's that Gif Garrison-Spouter Powell crowd that did it," muttered Slugger Brown. "I saw 'em working like troopers to defeat us."

"Yes. And those Rover boys worked against both of you, too," piped in Codfish, who was present. "I watched 'em do it. They went all around among the fellows they know electioneering for the others who were running."

"It would be just like them to do it," muttered Nappy Martell, gloomily.

"I thought you were going to fight that Jack Rover to a finish some day?" questioned the sneak of the school.

"So I am—when I get the chance," returned Martell.

As soon as the election of officers was settled, the minds of a certain number of cadets turned to football. Gif Garrison was busy arranging his teams and placing the names of the players up on a big board in the gymnasium.

"Hurrah!" shouted Fred, bursting in on Jack one afternoon while the latter was busy in his room studying the next day's lessons. "Our names are up on the board, Jack! Gif has put us up for a try-out on the scrub eleven!"

"Is that so!" exclaimed his cousin, his face showing his satisfaction. "Are you sure?"

"I am. I just came from the gymnasium. We are to report for practice to-morrow afternoon at four o'clock."

"Is Andy or Randy up?"

"No. You remember they told Gif they didn't want to play football this season."

The Rover boys soon learned that not only Gif but also Spouter, Ned Lowe, Walt Baxter, and Slugger Brown were on the regular eleven. The scrub team was made up largely from the freshmen class, although Dan Soppinger and a few others of the older cadets who had never played on the first team were also included.

"Now, I want all of you to do your very best," said Gif, at the close of a long talk to the boys on what was required of them. "We'll have nothing but squad work first, and then a game or two just to find out how matters are shaping themselves."

As an aid Gif had Mr. Crews, the gymnasium instructor, who in his younger days had been quite a football player. Between the pair matters took shape rapidly, and by the end of the week the scrub was in shape to play a game against the regulars.

As was to be expected, this opening contest was a decidedly ragged one, even the regular team making many plays which caused hearty laughter.

"You fellows have all got to do better if we want to win any matches," declared Gif. "Now then, go at it as if you meant it and see that you mind the rules." And after that the playing showed gradual improvement.

Colonel Colby had not forgotten his own football days, and one afternoon he came down to the field to see what progress his pupils were making.

"Be on the alert when the signals are given," he said. "The signals," he added, "count for a good deal."

With the master of the school present, the cadets put forth renewed efforts and the playing became actually snappy. There were several well-earned runs, and once Jack managed to kick a goal from the field which brought forth considerable applause.

"Keep it up, Jack! You're doing fine!" were Gif's encouraging words.

"Thanks. I'll do the best I know how," was the rejoinder.

Fred was also working hard, and a little later he made a run which netted the scrub team fifteen yards.

"Fine! Fine!" cried his cousin encouragingly.

"That was well played," announced Gif. "But I want every man on the field to do better than he has been doing," he added, stiffening up, for he knew that a captain can only get out of his men the best that is in them by thus urging them on.

During several of the plays Jack had come into contact with Slugger Brown, and the big fellow showed that he had no friendly feeling for the Rover boy.

"You be careful," warned Jack, when Brown started once to

tackle him unfairly. But the big fellow merely grinned in a sarcastic fashion. Then, less than two minutes later and while there was a wild rush on, Slugger Brown, by a sidelong and unexpected leap, hurled Jack to the ground and spiked him in the leg with his shoe.

CHAPTER XVIII

SLUGGER BROWN IS EXPOSED

To be thrown down so violently was bad enough, but to be spiked in the leg hurt so much that Jack could not repress a gasp of pain.

"Get off of me, Brown!" he panted when he could speak. "What do you mean by spiking me that way?"

"Didn't spike you!" retorted Slugger Brown, scowling viciously.

The whistle blew and Gif came running towards the pair. "What's the matter?" he demanded.

"Brown tackled me unfairly and then spiked me," answered Jack.

"It's false!" roared the accused one. "I threw him down according to the rules and I didn't spike him at all!"

The pain in Jack's leg was so intense that he could hardly stand. Fred and some others came rushing to his assistance, and between them he managed to hobble to a bench at the side of the football field. A crowd began to collect, and all

Arthur M. Winfield

wanted to know what had gone wrong.

"Let us take a look at your leg, Rover," said Mr. Crews. "That will show whether you were spiked or not." The limb was exposed, and then a cry of dismay went up.

"Why, look there—it's all bloody! Slugger Brown must have spiked him for keeps!"

"That's a shame—if he did it on purpose. He has no right to have spikes in his shoes."

"I didn't do it on purpose! It was an accident!" cried the accused player. "I didn't know I had spiked him or that I had spikes. Maybe he cut himself on a stone or something like that."

"No; he has been spiked," announced the gymnasium instructor, after examining the wound. "Come, Rover; we'll go to the gymnasium and I'll attend to that and bind it up for you."

"You ought to be ashamed of yourself, Brown, for doing such a thing to my cousin," said Fred.

"That's right!" broke in Randy, who had come up.

"You stop your talking!" answered Slugger Brown, uneasily. "It was an accident, I tell you. Anybody on the team might have done it."

Colonel Colby had been on the other side of the field, but now he came hurrying forward to see what was amiss. He told Mr. Crews to do everything that was necessary for Jack, and then turned to Gif.

"I think it would be as well for you to retire Brown for the present," he said in a low voice.

"Just what I was going to do," answered the football captain quickly. "We'll have to investigate this matter after the game is over."

"I don't see why I should be put off the team!" cried Slugger Brown, when notified that a substitute would take his place. "It was an accident and nothing else."

"We'll see about that later, Brown," answered Gif briefly. "Anyway, you had no right to have spikes on your shoes."

With one substitute in place of Brown and another playing Jack's position, the game went on and came to a finish in favor of the regular team by a score of 22 to 16.

"Not such a very good showing for the regulars," was Gif's comment.

"Maybe, if Jack had been in shape to play, we might have beaten you," remarked Fred, grimly.

"Oh, I'm not willing to admit that," answered the football captain. "Just the same, some of you fellows on the scrub did very well, indeed. I'm going to continue to keep my eyes on all of you."

Down in the gymnasium the wound inflicted by the spikes in Slugger Brown's shoe had been carefully washed and dressed by Mr. Crews and then bandaged.

"I don't think you'll have any great trouble from it, Rover," remarked the gymnasium instructor. "But, just the same, you had better favor that leg for a few days."

Arthur M. Winfield

"Then you wouldn't advise me to play football?" questioned Jack in dismay.

"Not for the next few days. After that I think you'll be all right."

As soon as the game was over, Gif, aided by Mr. Crews, began an investigation, closely questioning all of the players and those looking on who had seen the encounter between Brown and Jack. Of course, there were various versions of the affair, but the consensus of opinions seemed to be that the tackle had been an unfair one and that Brown could have avoided spiking Jack had he been more careful. It was likewise considered unfair to use spiked shoes even in a practice game.

"I guess he did it just to be nasty," said Gif to Mr. Crews. "You see, he and Nappy Martell and that crowd are all down on the Rovers."

"I know nothing about the quarrels between the cadets," was Mr. Crews' reply. "But I do know that spiking anyone on purpose cannot be permitted in this institution. I recommend, Garrison, that Brown be suspended from the team."

This was going a little further than Gif had anticipated. He knew that Brown was a fairly good player, carrying considerable weight, and that the cadet's heart would be almost broken if he was taken out of the games entirely.

"Don't you think, Mr. Crews, it would be going far enough if I put him on the bench with the substitutes?" he pleaded. "To be thrown out of the team entirely is a terrible blow for any one."

"But we expect our cadets to act like young gentlemen and

not like brutes, Garrison," returned the gymnastic instructor warmly. "However, if you wish to place Brown among the substitutes, I will not oppose you. His weight might help you to win some game if it was running very close and some of your best players dropped out." And so it was arranged.

Slugger Brown had been very anxious to know what the outcome of the matter would be. He was far from appeased when he received the notification that, while he would be retained on the regular team, it would be only as a substitute.

"A substitute, eh?" he said sarcastically to Gif. "So that is the way you are going to punish me for something that couldn't be helped."

"Mr. Crews and I went into the details of the affair, Brown," answered the football captain. "Mr. Crews wanted to put you off the team entirely. It was only through my efforts that you are to remain as a substitute."

"I've been the mainstay of our football eleven ever since it was organized!" stormed Slugger Brown. "I helped to win every victory that came our way."

"I'm not denying that you play well. But, just the same, if you'll remember, you've been warned of your brutal attacks before. In that game with Hixley High last Fall, the left tackle said, if you will remember, that you ought to be handed over to the police. Now Mr. Crews says—and I agree with him—that we've got to play in a clean-cut fashion, free from all needless brutality."

"Bah! I won't listen to you," howled Slugger Brown. "You're in with those Rovers, and that whole crowd is down on me just because I am chummy with Nappy Martell. I won't stand for it! If I can't play on the regular team, I won't play at all!"

"Very well then, you can suit yourself about that," answered Gif; and to avoid further argument he walked away, leaving the big youth in anything but a pleasant frame of mind.

The interview had taken place in the gymnasium, and presently Slugger Brown was joined by Nappy Martell and three or four other cronies, including Codfish.

"It's an outrage!" was Martell's comment, when Slugger had told of what had occurred. "I wouldn't stand for it! No wonder you told him you wouldn't play on the eleven any more."

"A team that has got a captain like that doesn't deserve to win," was the comment of one of the other cadets.

"Say, Slugger, why don't you get to work and see if you can't boost Gif Garrison out of his place? He has no more right to be captain of the eleven than you have."

"Easy enough to say," growled Brown. "But Garrison has too many of the fellows under his thumb. Oh, I don't care—they can go to grass with their old football games!" And then Slugger Brown stalked off by himself to nurse his wrath as best he could. He was very bitter against Jack.

"It's all that Rover boy's fault," he muttered to himself. "I don't wonder Nappy is down on that crowd."

The recent cold snap had given way to weather that was quite balmy; and, being unable to put in his off time in football practice, Jack remembered what he had said to Ruth Stevenson about a row on the river. He consulted with Fred, and then the pair managed to get a message to both Ruth and May Powell; and in return received word that the two girls would be pleased to go out the following afternoon about four o'clock.

"Gee! you fellows will have a dandy time," remarked Randy, when he heard of this. "Why didn't you let us know?"

"Four in one of those rowboats is about enough," answered Jack. "But if you and Andy want to go out, why don't you get another boat and send word to a couple of the other girls?"

"All right! Let's do it," answered Andy, quickly; and the upshot of the matter was that they telephoned over to Clearwater Hall and made an arrangement with Alice Strobell and Annie Larkins.

"It's a shame we can't ask Jennie Mason, too," said Randy, who remembered the fifth girl who had been in the crowd at the moving picture theater.

"You won't have to worry about Jennie," answered Alice Strobell, over the telephone. "She has a date with somebody else."

The Rover boys had already arranged about the boats, and promptly on time they set off down the river in the direction of the lake. They had to row past the several docks of the town, and then drew up at a small wharf, leading up to the Clearwater Hall grounds.

When the girls appeared, they were accompanied by one of the teachers, who had been sent down, evidently, for the purpose of looking the cadets over.

"Now remember, do not stay out any later than six o'clock," said the teacher, as the girls were entering the two rowboats, assisted by the boys.

"Oh, we'll have to come back a little before that time," answered Jack. "You see, we are due at Colby Hall at that hour."

"Very well then," said the teacher. "I trust you all have a pleasant time," and she smiled.

"Oh, we'll have a good time—don't worry," sang out Andy, gaily.

"To be sure we will," echoed May Powell.

And then, with the girls safely seated in the two rowboats, the boys took up the oars, and the little outing on Clearwater Lake was begun.

CHAPTER XIX

A SQUALL ON THE LAKE

"It's too bad we don't happen to have a motor boat up here," remarked Jack, as he and Fred bent to the oars of their rowboat.

"You mustn't work too hard," came from Ruth.

"I wasn't thinking of that," answered the oldest Rover boy quickly. "I was only thinking if we had a motor boat we could go farther."

"They are going to have a motor boat or two at Colby Hall next Spring—I heard Colonel Colby speaking about it," put in Fred.

"That will be very fine," remarked May. "I suppose you'll give us a ride once in a while?" she added, her eyes twinkling.

"Sure!" responded the youngest Rover, quickly.

"Hi—over there!" came from Andy, as he and his twin bent to the oars. "Want to race?"

Arthur M. Winfield

"Of course—if you'd like to!" responded Jack.

"Oh, a race!" exclaimed Alice Strobell. "Won't that be fine!"

"There won't be any danger, will there?" questioned Annie Larkins, anxiously.

"No danger whatever, so long as we keep far enough apart," answered Randy. "And we'll do that, because we expect to leave them far behind."

"Not much you won't leave us behind!" retorted Fred. And then he added: "Are you ready?"

"Wait a minute until we have the young ladies seated just right," answered Andy. And then, turning to the two girls in the boat with him, he continued gaily: "Now sit right in the center of the boat, please; and be sure to have your hair parted exactly in the middle;" and at this both girls shrieked with laughter.

With their passengers seated to their satisfaction, the four Rovers prepared for the race.

"Where are we going to race to?" questioned Jack.

"I don't know," answered Randy. "Can any of you tell me?" he went on, appealing to the pupils from Clearwater Hall.

"You might race to the near end of Foxtail Island," suggested Ruth, and pointed to an island some distance down the lake.

"That suits!" cried Jack.

"The first one to reach the dock at the end of the island wins the race," announced May.

"And what's the prize?" questioned Fred.

"Oh, the prize will be the pleasure of rowing back," answered May, and at this little joke there was a general laugh.

"Now please don't tip us overboard," pleaded Alice.

"Nary a tip," answered Randy.

"We're not looking for tips," broke in Andy, quickly. "We are going to do this free, gratis, for nothing," and at this pun there was another laugh. Then Jack gave the signal, and away the two rowboats started on the race.

Of course, it was only a friendly affair, and none of the boys rowed as hard as he would have done in a regular contest. Nevertheless, each craft made good progress over the sparkling waters of the lake.

"Oh, my! you certainly can row," remarked Ruth to Jack and Fred, as their craft drew ahead.

"Oh, we're not warmed up yet," was Jack's reply.

"We could do much better if we were in regular rowing togs," explained Fred.

"Hi you! What do you mean by going ahead?" piped out Randy. "Come on, Andy, or they'll beat us."

"Maybe they can beat a drum, but they can't beat us," cried Andy.

And then he and his twin increased their strokes so that presently their boat was once more beside the other.

The girls were as much interested as the boys in the impromptu race, and they soon began to shout words of encouragement.

"Pull! pull! we're going to win!" cried May.

"Not a bit of it! Our boat will get there first!" sang out Alice.

"You can't beat us!" came from Annie.

"He crows best who crows last," cried Ruth.

"Right you are!" came pantingly from Jack; and then, as he saw the look of encouragement in Ruth's face, he redoubled his efforts. Fred did the same, and when they came into plain view of the tiny dock at the end of Foxtail Island their boat was two full lengths ahead of the other.

"Hi you! What kind of a race is this, anyhow?" shouted out Andy, gaily. "Why don't you keep side by side and be sociable?"

"Sour grapes!" roared Fred. "Here is where we win!" and in a moment more he and Jack sent their boat up to the side of the little dock. Almost immediately the second craft followed.

"I think all of you did very well," remarked Ruth, consolingly.

"Anyway, we came in a close second," remarked Randy.

"We would have won if it hadn't been for one thing—just one thing," remarked Andy, solemnly.

"Why, what was that?" questioned several of the others quickly.

"That was the fact that the other boat"—Andy drew a deep breath—"came in first." At this the girls shrieked with laughter and the other boys set up a howl.

"Pitch him into the lake!"

"That's right! Give him a bath!"

"A ducking will do him good—he needs to be cooled off!"

"Not much! No bath for me!" cried Andy, quickly, and lost no time in leaping to the dock, where, in the exuberance of his spirits, he turned several handsprings, much to the amusement of the girls.

"Is there anything worth seeing on this island?" questioned Jack, when the excitement of the race was over.

"There isn't anything here that I know of," answered Ruth. "In the summer time people come here to picnic. There is a nice spring of water in the center of the island."

"Let's go and get a drink," said Fred. "That race made me thirsty;" and off the whole party trooped to the spring.

The young folks had a good time at the spring and in exploring the little island, which had a hill at one end covered with trees. They found some chestnuts and also a few hickory nuts, and these the boys opened for the girls' benefit.

"I suppose we had better go on and finish the row," remarked Jack to Ruth, presently. "That is, unless you girls would rather wander through the woods."

"Oh, it's nice enough here on the island," she answered.

Arthur M. Winfield

"Remember, you'll have quite a row back to the school and then to Colby Hall."

"Oh, let's stay here for a while," put in Alice. "Maybe we'll be able to find more nuts."

They hunted around, and presently discovered another large chestnut tree which was fairly loaded. The boys threw up sticks and stones, and brought down a big shower.

"If I had known this, we might have brought along a pillowcase for the nuts," said Fred.

"We can come back some day if we want to," returned Randy.

Before leaving the island the young folks decided to go back to where the spring was located, so as to get another drink and also to wash their hands. On this trip, in speaking about the excitement at the moving picture theater, Randy chanced to mention Jennie Mason's name.

"Jennie is a nice girl," answered Annie Larkins, to whom he was speaking, "but she does some things that I do not approve of. Do you know a cadet at your Hall named Napoleon Martell—I think they call him Nappy for short?"

"Do we know him!" exclaimed Randy. "I should say we did!"

"Oh! is that so?" Annie looked at him searchingly. "Is he a friend of yours?"

"No; I can't say that he is. To tell you the truth, he doesn't like us at all."

"If that's the case, I don't mind speaking to you about Jennie," went on the girl. "You know, Jennie comes from New York City. And down there she met Nappy Martell quite a few times, and they became well acquainted. But Jennie's folks don't approve of him at all; and they don't want her to go with him." And here Annie paused.

"And do you mean to say she does go with him, anyhow?" queried the Rover boy.

"Yes. She goes out to meet him whenever she can get the chance," was the reply. "You are sure you don't approve of him?"

"Not in the least. In fact, to tell the truth, we have no use for him or the bunch he trains with."

"I see. Well, all of us think it is perfectly dreadful the way Jennie accepts Martell's invitations. Of course, we don't want to tell on her, either in school or to her folks, and yet none of us think it is right."

"Does he take her out much?"

"Oh, as much as they dare to go. He takes her out sailing on the lake and to the moving picture shows, and once they went off together on a picnic to the Clearwater Country Club. The places were all right in themselves, but I know Jennie's folks don't want her to be seen in the company of Nappy Martell. He is so loud and forward."

"You can't tell us anything about Martell being loud and forward," answered Randy, readily. "We all know him to be a regular bully. Besides that, when he isn't in uniform, he wears the loudest kind of clothes—just as if he wanted to make an exhibition of himself."

"Jennie went out with him this afternoon," continued Annie. "Where they went to, I do not know. But I think they hired a motor boat and went across the lake."

"Does Martell know how to run a motor boat?"

"Oh, yes. He told Jennie that he owned a motor boat on the Hudson River—a boat his father gave him for a birthday present."

Randy and the girl had dropped a little behind the others, who now waited for them to come up.

"I think we had better be getting back," said Jack. "It isn't as clear as it was before, and it is beginning to blow."

"Yes, we'll get back," returned Randy, with a look at the sky. He knew that a blow on the lake might be no trifling matter.

On the way over to the island the sun had been clear and warm. Now, however, it was hidden under a dark bank of clouds, which were coming up quickly from the west. The wind was already blowing freely, and out on the bosom of the lake the water was roughing up in tiny ripples.

"All aboard, everybody!" sang out Jack. And then turning to his cousins he added in a low voice: "We mustn't lose a minute of time in getting back. This blow is going to be a heavy one."

The girls were soon seated in the rowboats, and then the four Rovers lost no time in casting off from the little dock and in starting to row towards Clearwater Hall. As they proceeded, the sky kept growing darker and darker while the wind grew stronger and stronger.

"We're in for a squall all right enough," murmured Randy, as he and Andy bent to their oars with vigor.

"Gee! I only hope we can reach the shore before it strikes us," was the response.

"Row for all you're worth, boys!" sang out Jack from the other boat. "Bend to it just as if you were in a race!"

And then he and Fred, as well as the twins, settled down to the task of trying to outrace the oncoming squall.

Arthur M. Winfield

CHAPTER XX

IN GREAT PERIL

As those who have had any experience know, a squall on a lake encircled by hills sometimes comes up very quickly, and this is what happened in the present case. Hardly had the two rowboats covered a quarter of the distance to the shore, when the wind came whistling across the bosom of the lake, sending the whitecaps tumbling in all directions.

"Oh, dear, just look how rough the water is getting!" remarked Ruth in alarm.

"And how the wind is blowing!" added May.

In the other boat the girls were even more fearful, and Andy and Randy had all they could do to make them sit still.

"Don't shift," pleaded Randy. "We don't want to ship any water."

"Oh, dear! If only we were safe on shore!" wailed Alice.

"I didn't think it looked like a storm when we left the school," added Annie, in dismay.

"This is only a squall. It may blow itself out in a few minutes," returned Randy, although to himself he admitted that the squall looked as though it might last for some time.

Battling as best they could against the wind and the whitecaps, the Rover boys strove to reach the shore in the vicinity of the girls' school. But the wind was blowing directly down Clearwater Lake and threatened more than once to capsize them.

"Gee, Jack, this is getting serious!" panted Fred, as he looked questioningly at his cousin.

The same thought had come into the minds of each of the boys. Could the girls swim? They wished they knew, but did not dare to ask any questions for fear of further alarming their passengers.

"I guess we had better head up into the wind. It's the safest thing to do," cried Jack. And then, raising his voice to be heard above the whistling of the elements, he added: "Head up! Don't take those waves sideways! Head up!"

The others understood, and in a minute more both of the boats were heading directly into the wind. This prevented either of the craft from swamping, but caused the spray to hit the bow more than once, sending a shower of water over everybody.

"Oh, dear! I'm getting wet!" wailed May.

"Do you think you can reach shore?" questioned Ruth of Jack; and her wide-open eyes showed her terror.

"We can't head for the school just now," he answered. "We'll have to keep pulling up against the wind until it lets up a little."

Arthur M. Winfield

"Oh, but we sha'n't upset, shall we?" came from Spouter Powell's cousin.

"I don't think so. Anyway, we are going to do our best to prevent it," answered Fred.

Keeping as close together as they dared, the two rowboats continued to head up into the wind, which still blew as hard as ever. In the sky the clouds were shifting, and Jack and his cousins had great hopes that ere long the sudden squall would blow itself out.

"Here comes a motor boat up behind us!" cried Ruth, presently.

All looked in that direction and saw a fair-sized craft coming up the lake. She was making good speed in spite of the whitecaps, and was sending the spray flying in all directions.

"I think that is the boat Jennie Mason was going out in," remarked Annie to Randy. "Yes; I am sure it is," she added a minute later, as the motor boat came closer. "There is Mr. Martell at the wheel now."

The discovery that Nappy Martell was running the oncoming motor boat had also been made by those occupying the other rowboat.

"It's Martell! And there is Slugger Brown with him!" cried Fred.

"Isn't one of those girls Miss Mason?" questioned Jack.

"Yes. And Ida Brierley, one of our girls, is with her," answered Ruth. Her manner indicated that the discovery did not altogether please her.

"Maybe we can get that motor boat to pull us in," suggested May. "They could do it easily enough."

"So they could," answered Fred. "But I doubt if those two fellows who are running it would like to undertake the job. They go to Colby Hall, but they are no friends of ours."

"Yes, but they ought not to let their enmity stand between us in a time like this," said Jack. "If they were in the rowboats and I was in the motor boat, I'd give them help quick enough."

As the motor boat drew nearer, it prepared to pass close to the craft manned by Jack and Fred. As it came closer, Jennie Mason gave a cry of surprise.

"Oh, look! look! There are those Rover boys, and some of our girls are with them!"

"I'm glad I am not out in a rowboat," said Ida Brierley. "I'd be afraid of getting a good ducking."

"Ahoy there, on the motor boat!" sang out Fred, as the craft came alongside. "Can't you fellows give us a tow? We have plenty of rope."

"This motor boat wasn't built for towing," answered Nappy Martell, roughly.

"We're having a terrible time of it against this wind," put in Jack. He would not have asked for assistance on his own account, but he was thinking of the girls. He knew that all of them were badly frightened.

"Oh, yes! please tow us in!" came from May.

"Yes! please do!" added Ruth.

"It's so far to the shore!" came from Annie.

"And we're afraid we'll get wet through and through!" cried Alice.

"You ought to do something for them," declared Jennie Mason, who had herself become frightened over the roughness of the lake.

"I'm not going to tow those Rovers in," muttered Nappy Martell. "You wouldn't do it, would you, Slugger?"

"Not much! Let 'em take care of themselves," was the heartless answer.

"Oh! but they may be drowned!" gasped Jennie.

"Nothing of the sort. This is only a little wind, and it will soon die down. If those Rovers have to break their backs rowing, it will do 'em good!"

"If you don't tow us in, you'll be the meanest fellow on earth," sang out Andy.

"I wouldn't have your disposition for a million dollars," added his twin.

"Aw! go chase yourselves!" retorted Slugger Brown, heartlessly.

"We're not helping fellows like you," came from Nappy Martell. Then the motor boat passed on and was soon all but lost in the distance.

"Of all the mean people!" cried Ruth.

"I shouldn't think Jennie Mason would stand for such meanness," declared May. "Nor Ida Brierley, either."

The motor boat having gone on and left them to their fate, the Rover boys continued pulling on the oars. It was hard, laborious work, and soon Andy and Fred were all but exhausted. Jack and Randy, however, had now gotten their second wind, so to speak, and they continued their efforts with unabated vigor.

"It was as mean as dirt for them to leave us out here when they could have towed us in with ease," panted Fred. "Just you wait—I'll let the whole school know of this!"

"Don't talk! Save your wind. We can talk afterwards," returned his cousin.

The next quarter of an hour was one which none of the girls or boys ever forgot. The Rovers continued to battle with the wind and the waves with all the energy left to them, while the girls crouched down on the seats almost speechless with fear. Occasionally, the waves would hit the bow of one rowboat or the other, sending a shower of water over the occupants.

"I—think—it's—letting up—a—bit," panted Jack, presently, and glanced up at the sky.

"Oh, if only it would!" breathed Ruth.

The boat containing the others had dropped slightly behind, but now Jack and Fred held back until it was once more alongside.

Arthur M. Winfield

"Oh, did you ever see such a storm!" wailed Alice.

"I don't think I'll ever want to go out in a rowboat again," was Annie's bitter comment.

"I think the wind is beginning to die down," said Ruth, encouragingly.

"Let—us—hope—so," came in jerks from Jack. He was still rowing, but his arms felt as if they were being torn from their sockets.

They had now covered nearly half the distance to the upper end of the lake, but they were just as far from the western shore as ever. Now, however, as the wind began to die down, they turned slightly in the direction of Haven Point.

"It won't matter where we land," declared Ruth. "We can easily walk back to the school."

The sun was still under a cloud, but now the wind went down more than ever. The surface of the lake, however, was still much troubled, and the boys had all they could do to make any progress towards the shore.

"Oh, you must be very tired!" said Ruth to Jack.

"Never—mind—we'll—reach—shore—somehow," he answered. Then she said no more, because she knew it was painful for him to speak.

The four boys continued to row on, and in about a quarter of an hour came within plain view of the shore, at a point some distance beyond Clearwater Hall and the town.

"Oh, look! Something is the matter down by the lumber

yards," remarked Alice, presently. "See the men running!" She pointed, and those in both rowboats looked in that direction.

"I don't see anything wrong," said Ruth.

"I do!" cried May, and gave a little shriek. "Look! look! A whole lot of lumber is drifting this way!"

"Some—thing—broken—lose," gasped Jack. "Maybe—a—lumber—raft."

And that was just what had happened. In a manner to be explained later, a lumber raft being towed up the lake by a steam tug had not only broken away, but likewise had broken apart, and the timbers which had composed it were now floating around over a large area of Clearwater Lake.

In another minute the two rowboats were in the very midst of the drifting timbers and in great danger of being upset.

Arthur M. Winfield

CHAPTER XXI

ASSISTANCE REFUSED

"My gracious! look at the lumber floating around!"

"Be careful, boys! Don't get hit if you can help it!"

"One of those timbers is heavy enough to send us to the bottom!"

"Oh, dear! Do you think we'll be smashed up?"

Such were some of the cries which rent the air as the Rover boys and the girls with them found themselves in the midst of the wreckage from the broken-apart lumber raft.

On all sides of them heavy sticks of timber were bobbing up and down on the whitecaps, and presently one of these bumped into the craft occupied by Jack and Fred and two of the girls. The rowboat careened so much that quite a large quantity of water was shipped, which made Ruth and May scream in fright.

"Stand up in the bow, Fred, and see if you—can—ward—them—off!" gasped Jack as well as his semi-exhausted condition would permit. "I'll stick to—the—oars."

He knew he must keep the rowboat headed up into the wind, for the squall had not yet subsided sufficiently to allow of their taking it sidewise.

A moment later came a cry from the other rowboat as the craft slipped up and over several large sticks of timber.

"Gosh! that was a narrow escape!" was Andy's comment, as the craft finally righted itself.

"Oh, dear! if only we were on shore once more!" wailed Annie, for at least the tenth time.

"I never dreamed that we would have such a dreadful experience as this!" came from Alice.

Randy said nothing, but continued to row, while Andy did the same as Fred was doing, both trying their best to ward off the heavy sticks which came floating towards them every minute or two.

Not far away was a steam tug, and presently two other boats came from the shore, both bent upon saving all that was possible of the broken-apart lumber raft.

"We'll pick you up if you have much trouble," cried the captain of the steam tug, as he ran a course between the two rowboats. "But don't ask us to do it unless it's necessary, for we want to round up this floating lumber before it gets away from us, if it can be done."

"Thank you!" gasped out Jack, in return. "Maybe we can—make—the—shore. The wind seems—to—be—going—down."

"Sure, we'll make it!" put in Randy. The fright of the girls in

Arthur M. Winfield

his boat had somewhat nettled him and he was resolved to land them safely without assistance.

But it was a time of peril as well as exhausting effort; and all of the Rovers were glad enough when the last of the drifting lumber was passed and they came within hailing distance of the shore. The wind had now gone down considerably, and most of this was to be felt farther out on the lake.

"Let us take them right down to the school dock," sang out Randy. "We can turn down the lake, and the wind will be just strong enough to help us;" and so it was arranged.

When the two rowboats came within sight of the school dock, those on board found fully a dozen of the scholars there, along with two of the teachers.

"Are you safe?" cried one of the teachers, as soon as the boats came within hailing distance.

"Yes, Miss Glover. We are all right," answered Ruth.

"Only we are rather wet," added May.

"And I'm awfully glad to get back," broke in Annie, who was fairly shivering over her trying experience.

"Well, anyway, I think you cadets did perfectly splendid," remarked Alice.

"Indeed they did!" broke out Ruth, quickly. "I don't believe anyone could have managed these boats better;" and she bestowed a glance of admiration first on Jack and then on his cousins.

"It was a terrible blow, and it came up so quickly that we all grew alarmed for your safety," said Miss Glover.

"And then to think that you must get mixed up with that drifting lumber!" put in the other teacher. "The squall was bad enough without having anything like that happen."

"It's too bad the lumbermen had their big raft go apart like that," was Jack's comment. "I guess those big sticks of timber are worth a good deal of money."

"They couldn't have had the raft chained together very tightly," said Miss Glover, who had come from a lumbering community where rafting was frequent. "I never heard of a raft going to pieces like that."

"Well, I don't know much about lumber rafts," answered Jack.

"Say, can't we leave our two rowboats here and ride back to the Hall?" questioned Randy. "I don't want to do any more rowing if I can help it."

"Of course you can leave your boats here," answered Miss Glover, and she showed where the craft might be stowed away in the boathouse. All of the Rovers were glad enough to give up further work at the oars.

"I am awfully sorry our little outing turned out as it did," remarked Jack to Ruth.

"And it was too bad to frighten you so," added Randy, to all of the girls.

"Oh, it wasn't your fault that the squall came up," answered Ruth. "And, besides that, now it is over I think I rather enjoyed the adventure—that is. I'll enjoy telling about it,"

Arthur M. Winfield

she corrected.

"Some day I hope we'll be able to spend a nicer time together," said Jack.

"Perhaps," murmured Ruth, and blushed.

Before the Rovers left for Colby Hall, they asked if Jennie Mason and Ida Brierley had returned.

"They have not come back yet," answered one of the teachers. "We saw them going up the lake against the wind. We were a little bit worried, but I presume the motor boat can take care of itself in quite a blow."

"All they've got to do is to turn on the gasolene, while in a rowboat sometimes a fellow's muscles give out," was Andy's comment, and this caused a smile.

After bidding the girls and the others good-bye, the four Rovers walked towards the town. There they were fortunate enough to find the Hall auto-stage, and were soon at the school once more.

"Gee! but my arms ache!" was Fred's remark on the way. "The muscles hurt so I can hardly keep still."

"You'd better bathe them well with witch hazel or alcohol," returned Jack. "My muscles feel sore, too."

"It took the wind right out of me," came from Andy. "Funny, too—with so much wind all around," he added merrily.

"I can't help but think of how Martell and Brown treated us," said Randy, seriously. "It was as mean as dirt!"

"I believe they would have left us there to drown!" added Fred.

"Oh, I wouldn't like to think that of them," broke in Jack. "Just the same, it was a very dirty thing to do. Not on our account so much as on account of the girls."

When the boys got back, the first person they met was Spouter, who wanted to know how his cousin May had enjoyed the outing. He listened in some alarm to the story the Rovers had to relate.

"It was a narrow shave all right," was the comment. And then his face took on a stern look. "And to think Nappy Martell and Slugger Brown treated you that way! Those fellows ought to be run out of this school!"

The squall on the lake had been noticed by some of the other cadets who had been out on the river; and the news soon spread of the danger into which the Rovers and their companions had run. Gif, Ned, Walt, and several others wanted to know the particulars of the affair, and all were loud in their denunciation of the cadets who had been running the motor boat.

"Spouter is right!" declared Gif. "Those fellows ought to be run out of Colby Hall!"

"After this I want nothing more to do with them!" added Ned.

"I wonder what they would say if some of you had been drowned," remarked Walt.

"Makes me want to pitch into 'em," came from Fatty, who was present. "But then, in one way, it's a pity to dirty one's hands on such cattle as that."

Of course, the Rover boys had come in late for supper. Professor Lemm had started to find fault with Andy and Fred for this, but he was quickly stopped by Colonel Colby, who had come up to learn the particulars of what had occurred.

"I heard you were out in that big blow," remarked the colonel. "I trust none of you suffered from it."

"Well, we had rather a narrow escape," answered Fred. Then he and Andy gave a brief outline of what had happened, not forgetting to mention how Martell and Brown had left them to their fate.

"Too bad! too bad!" murmured the colonel, shaking his head slightly. "I did not think that any of our cadets would do such a thing;" and then he walked away in a very thoughtful mood.

"I wonder what he'll say to Brown and Martell," mused Fred, as, after being dismissed by Professor Lemm, they hurried to the mess hall. As they were late, they had missed the parade.

"Maybe he'll give 'em a piece of his mind. I hope he does," answered his cousin.

Nappy Martell and Slugger Brown did not appear until supper was almost over. Both had a gloomy look, as if something had gone decidedly wrong. They glared sourly at the Rover boys and their chums, and then sat down to their meal without saying a word to anybody.

"I'll wager something slipped a cog with them," whispered Fred to Jack.

"I've got an idea," returned the oldest of the Rover boys. "Maybe Jennie Mason and that other girl who were out in the motor boat gave them a piece of their mind for not aiding us."

"Oh, I hope they did, Jack!"

"It wouldn't be anything to wonder at. That Jennie Mason seemed to be a nice girl, and I don't think she would stand for any such meanness."

Jack's surmise concerning what had happened to Nappy and Slugger was correct. The two girls had pleaded with the two cadets to go back and give those in the rowboats aid. And after much argument, in which Nappy and Slugger had proved that they were anything but young gentlemen, the girls had politely asked to be taken ashore. This had brought on something of a quarrel, and in the end the two cadets had taken the girls to a dock near the lumber yards and quite a distance from Clearwater Hall.

"Now you can have the fun of walking to the school," had been Nappy Martell's final words.

"And I don't think you'll go out with us again in a hurry," Slugger Brown had added.

"I'll never go out with you again," Ida Brierley had answered.

"And I'd much prefer to walk to the school alone than to ride any further with you in the motor boat," Jennie Mason had added; and thus the four had parted, the two girls resolving in their hearts never to have anything more to do with Nappy Martell and Slugger Brown.

Arthur M. Winfield

CHAPTER XXII

THE MEETING WITH HIXLEY HIGH

Football talk now filled the air at Colby Hall, and for the time being most of the cadets forgot about how the Rovers had been treated on the lake by Nappy Martell and Slugger Brown.

Nappy was particularly angry, because of the way he had been treated by Jennie Mason, on whom he had been sweet ever since they had become acquainted. Slugger, too, was hurt over what the girls had said about his meanness. But he was far more put out over the fact that he could act only as a substitute on the regular eleven, and that Gif Garrison had finally concluded to put Jack in his place. Fred had not won out for the first eleven, but Gif had told him he stood so high on the scrub that he might possibly make the team before the season came to an end.

"It's all those Rovers' fault," growled Slugger Brown to Martell.

"Of course it is!" was the unreasonable reply. "I'll tell you, Slug, we ought to do something to get square with those chaps."

"If I break loose and do that, it'll be something they'll remember as long as they live!" declared Slugger Brown, vehemently.

Nappy Martell looked at his crony knowingly, and then glanced around to see if anybody was listening.

"Let's do it right now, Slug," he said in a low voice. "I don't care what it is, so long as we can get the best of those Rovers."

"We'll think it over, Nap. This isn't to be any one-cent, every-day affair, you know."

"Right you are! I'm game for anything—just remember that!" added the other cadet.

As Gif Garrison had said, there were three football games scheduled for Colby Hall that Fall. The first of these was to be with Hixley High School, located in a town at the other end of the lake. Then would follow a game of more importance with the Clearwater Country Club, at their beautiful grounds on the outskirts of Haven Point. And then the last and most important game of all—that with Columbus Academy, located about ten miles away. Whether the last named game would be played at Colby Hall or at the Columbus Academy grounds, was still a question.

In a few days Jack recovered completely from the spiking he had received from Slugger Brown, and then he went at his football practice with greater vigor than ever. He took Slugger's place on the regular eleven, as already mentioned, and in his first game they beat the scrub team by a score of 32 to 12.

"Now, that's better!" declared Gif. "You didn't let the scrub

Arthur M. Winfield

walk all over you."

Fred had been on the scrub team, and, although that eleven had been defeated, he was in a rather happy frame of mind, for the reason that out of the twelve points scored he had been directly responsible for six points.

"I think Fred is going some," remarked Jack to Gif, later on when he had a chance to speak to the football captain privately.

"You're right, Jack," was the answer. "And I've got my eye on him."

The game with Hixley High was not a very important one, yet it was made the occasion for quite a gala day by not only the boys of both schools but likewise the girls attending the high school and also the young ladies of Clearwater Hall. The Rover boys and some of their chums invited Ruth and her several friends, including Jennie Mason and Ida Brierley, to be present, and this invitation was gladly accepted.

"I don't wonder that Slugger Brown and Nappy Martell look so glum occasionally," remarked Spouter to Jack the day after the invitations had been given and accepted. "I just had a talk with my cousin May, and she says Jennie Mason and Ida Brierley are through with those two cadets. They told Nappy and Slugger they thought they were nothing but cowards for the way they treated you Rovers on the lake."

"Well, I'm glad they've given up going with that pair," announced Jack.

The last game with Hixley High had been played on the grounds of that institution, so that the game this year was to take place at Colby Hall.

"You fellows will have the honor of bringing the girls over from Clearwater Hall," remarked Jack to his cousins and his chums. "I'll have to stay here and do a bit of practising."

The auto-stage and a number of automobiles and carriages had been requisitioned, and also a number of motor boats on the lake, and in these the young folks from Hixley High School and from Clearwater Hall journeyed to Colby Hall.

Jack was on the lookout for Ruth and the others, and lost no time in greeting the girl as soon as she appeared.

"I'm so glad that you're on hand to encourage us to win," said he, as he took Ruth's hand.

"Thank you. But how are you sure I am here to encourage you?" she questioned mischievously. "Maybe I'm going to root for Hixley High."

"You dare!" he returned earnestly, and then they both laughed and hurried towards the grandstand, where seats had been reserved for the entire party.

"Whoop her up for Hixley High!" was the cry. And then those in favor of the high school took up the slogan:

"Do or die!
Hixley High! Hixley High!"

"They mean to win if yelling will do it," was May Powell's comment.

"Oh, I guess the cadets of Colby Hall can yell, too," responded Fred. And he was right, for a moment later there boomed out this refrain:

Arthur M. Winfield

"Who are we?
Can't you see?
Colby Hall!
Dum! Dum! Dum, dum, dum!
Here we come with fife and drum!
Colby! Colby! Colby Hall!"

And this the cadets repeated over and over again until they were hoarse.

"Well, I've got to go now," said Jack, reluctantly, as word came for the team to gather in the dressing room for final instructions.

"Good-bye then," said Ruth, sweetly. And then, looking Jack full in the eyes, she added earnestly: "Oh, I do hope you'll win!"

They were simple words, but the way in which they were spoken, and the look that accompanied them, thrilled the youth to the heart, and he went down to the dressing room on feet that seemed to be walking on air.

"Now then, boys, I expect every one of you to do his level best," said Gif. "Hixley High has been bragging everywhere that it has a superior team this year and is going to walk all over us. I want you to play with vigor from the very start;" and then followed a number of directions concerning plays and signals, to all of which his eleven listened earnestly.

When the Colby Hall team came forth, they were given a loud round of applause, and this was repeated when Hixley High showed itself. The high school boys were nearly all seniors, and a glance sufficed to show that, player for player, they were quite a few pounds heavier than the cadets.

"If our eleven wins this game they will be going some," was Fatty's whispered comment to a fellow cadet.

"You're right there," was the answer. "Those chaps certainly look pretty husky."

It is not my intention here to give the particulars of this game with Hixley High, interesting as it proved to be. It was not the big game of the season—that was to come later. During the first quarter, the playing on both sides was rather rough and ragged, each school doing its best to wear its opponent out at the very start. In these onslaughts the weight carried by Hixley High told, so that when the whistle blew the score was 6 to 3.

"Hurrah! Hurrah!" came from the supporters of the high school. And again and again they boomed out with their slogan.

"This game isn't over yet!" cried one of the followers of Colby Hall.

"We haven't begun to play yet! Just watch us in the second half!" added another cadet.

"Oh, dear! I thought Colby Hall would score, sure!" pouted Ruth.

"Those Hixley High boys are awfully big fellows," answered May.

The second quarter opened with a good deal of cheering for each side. The playing now became more settled, and the ball went back and forth from the 20-yard line on one side to the 30-yard line on the other. Then came a mix-up, in the midst of which Jack managed to get the ball and start with it for the goal.

"Rover has it!"

"Run, Jack, run! Leg it for all you're worth!"

And Jack did run, making the best of his opportunity. Three of the Hixley High players did their utmost to down him, but when the third laid him low, he was directly over the chalk mark.

"A touchdown!" was the cry from the Colby Hall cadets. And then they gave vent to their feelings by tooting their horns and sounding their rattles.

The touchdown was followed by a skilful kick for goal, and with this in their favor, Colby Hall went at the game with renewed vigor, so that when the whistle blew for the ending of the second half the score stood 13 to 6 in favor of Colby Hall.

"That's the way to do it!"

"Keep it up, boys!"

"Oh, wasn't that a splendid run by Jack?" cried Ruth, enthusiastically.

"It certainly was!" answered one of the other girls.

With the score piling up against them, Hixley High grew fairly frantic in the third quarter. As a consequence, their play became rougher than ever, and twice they had to be called to order, and once they were penalized. But their vigor told, and in spite of all Colby Hall could do to hold them back, they gained constantly, and when the end of the third quarter was reached the score was a tie.

"Thirteen to thirteen! What do you think of that?"

"Some playing, eh?"

Each side cheered its own, but many were the anxious faces when the two elevens lined up for the final quarter.

"Now then, boys, dig into them!" cried Mr. Crews, earnestly. "Show them what Colby Hall can do!"

"Watch 'em—watch 'em closely!" cautioned Gif. "They may try to pull off some new stunt at the last minute."

Once more the two teams went at it "hammer and tongs." It was certainly a battle royal, and on more than one occasion it looked as if some of the players might be seriously injured. As it was, Hixley High had to put in one substitute, and Colby Hall took on two. But the fighting blood of the cadets was now up, and with a great rush they carried the ball over the Hixley High line. They failed, however, to kick the goal, much to the regret of their followers.

"Never mind, boys," said Gif, encouragingly. "Hold 'em now! That is all I ask of you—hold 'em!"

And hold them Colby did, although the high school lads fought like demons to carry the ball across the cadets' territory. Back and forth went the play, the crowd meanwhile yelling itself hoarse. The ball was on the Colby Hall 15-yard line when the whistle blew and the game was over.

"Colby Hall wins!"

"Hurrah! Hurrah!"

Arthur M. Winfield

Then the horns and rattles sounded out louder than ever, and in a twinkling the football field was alive with visitors, and the triumphant eleven was surrounded.

CHAPTER XXIII

TARGET PRACTICE

Colby Hall prepared for a great celebration that night in honor of their victory over Hixley High. Boxes and barrels had been stored away in anticipation of just such an occasion, and these were brought out and stacked up at a safe place along the river front.

"Bonfires to-night—and big ones, too!" cried Andy, and let off his surplusage of spirits by turning several handsprings.

"Look out, Andy!" cried Fred, "or some circus will capture you."

"Sour grapes!" retorted the fun-loving youth.

"Oh, it was grand—the way you held Hixley High back in that last quarter!" remarked Ruth to Jack. "I was so afraid they would break through and score, I could hardly wait for the whistle to blow."

"It was certainly some game!" answered Jack. "You see, they are so much heavier than we are."

The victorious eleven came in for all sorts of congratulations, and Jack was slapped on the back until the wind was almost knocked out of him. As soon as he could escape from his friends, he and the others took the girls down to a waiting automobile and set off for Clearwater Hall. On the way the young folks sang and cut up to their hearts' content, having the best possible time.

The only cadet at Colby Hall who was not elated over the victory was Slugger Brown. Even though two substitutes had been used in the game, and even though the big fellow had repented of his former decision, and agreed to play if called upon, Gif had ignored him and used a player at least ten pounds lighter in weight.

"He doesn't intend to give me a show—and that's all there is to it," remarked Slugger to Nappy Martell, bitterly.

"Well, you told him you wouldn't play unless you could go out at the start of the game," answered his crony.

"I told him that first, but afterwards I agreed to go in as a sub," growled Brown. "But I can see how it is—those Rovers have told Garrison how we acted on the lake, and so Garrison has made up his mind to ignore me entirely, even though I've got the weight and can play as good as any of them."

"Oh, I don't doubt but what it's the Rovers' fault!" retorted Martell. "And that puts me in mind—are we going to do anything to get square or not?"

"Don't worry about that, Nap—we'll do something all right enough! But I want the chance first to think up something that will be worth while," answered Slugger Brown, emphatically.

The bonfires along the river were lit directly after supper, after the cadets had received permission from Colonel Colby. The boys were allowed to do about as they pleased, the only stipulation being that they should avoid anything that might be dangerous or ungentlemanly.

With the bonfires blazing high, throwing a lurid glare over the campus and parade grounds, the cadets sang and danced and then started an impromptu parade which took them around the various buildings of the school. Many carried torches, while four had drums and bugles. There was a good deal of horseplay, and also something in the way of hazing.

"Here is where we get back at Codfish for some of his meanness!" cried Randy, as he and some of the others caught the sneak.

Then Codfish was made to stand up on an unusually large barrel and sing, after which he was told to hold out each hand for a valuable present.

"I don't want any present! I want to get down!" cried the sneak.

"Oh, this is something very valuable, Codfish," returned Randy, and winked at some of the others.

Just for the fun of it, some of the cadets had obtained some potatoes from the storehouse and started to roast these under one of the bonfires. Two of the potatoes, quite hot and black, were brought forth and thrust into Codfish's hands.

"Ouch! What do you mean by handing me red-hot potatoes!" yelled the sneak, in alarm.

"Oh, we thought you were hungry," cried one of the other cadets.

"You wanted to burn me—that's what you wanted to do!" shrieked Codfish, who, however, was far more scared than hurt. "I want to get down!"

"You've got to give us a dance first, Codfish," ordered Randy.

"That's right! Give us a jig!" put in Andy.

"Make it a Boston seven-step," suggested Jack.

"Or a Washington dip," added Fred.

A dozen of the cadets were shouting at poor Codfish to dance, and presently the excited boy commenced to shuffle his feet.

"Now jump up three times and we'll let you go!" cried Randy.

Codfish made one leap into the air and came down on the barrel top successfully. Then he tried a second leap, but, as Randy well knew, the barrel top was weak, and, with a crash, poor Codfish went down straight into the big barrel up to his armpits.

"Whoop! Codfish has busted the barrel!" cried Fred.

"What do you mean by breaking up housekeeping like that, Codfish?" demanded Andy.

"Let's do the baker act for him," went on Randy, quickly.

"The baker act?" queried several of the cadets. "What's that?"

"Don't you know the baker loves his rolls?" answered Andy,

with a broad grin.

"That's the talk!" came in a shout. "Let's give Codfish a roll;" and before the sneak could save himself the barrel was tipped up on its side and sent rolling over and over towards the parade ground.

"Ouch! Let up! I'll be killed!" screamed the victim. "This barrel may have a lot of nails in it!"

"Oh, do you think that's true?" asked one of the cadets in fright.

"Nary a nail! I saw to that before we used the barrel," answered Randy. "Such a rolling won't hurt him a bit;" and the cadets continued their sport with the barrel, finally sending it down a slight hill in the direction of the river. Here it lodged against some bushes, and Codfish was allowed to crawl forth. At once he took to his heels and disappeared.

It was noticed by many that Slugger Brown and Nappy Martell had not participated in the festivities of the evening. The two had gone off for a walk, during which they smoked many cigarettes and talked over their grievances against the Rovers. On their return they were met by Codfish, who related to them his tale of woe.

"Oh, we've got to do something," was Nappy Martell's comment. "If we don't, before we know it the Rovers will be fairly running this school."

"Well, they won't run me," growled Slugger Brown.

The following Monday found the Rover boys once more hard at work over their studies. They had now settled down to the regular routine of the Hall, and were doing very well,

Arthur M. Winfield

not only in their classes, but also in their training as young soldiers. Each of them could march and handle a gun as well as anybody, and now they were given the privilege of practising at target shooting—something which interested them greatly.

"Let's get up a little match among ourselves," said Randy one day; and this was agreed upon, eight new cadets entering the contest.

The shooting was done at a target set up against a tree some distance behind the gymnasium building; and the boys did their practising under the direction of Captain Dale.

"It requires considerable practice to become an expert shot," said the military instructor. "Once in a while we find someone who is a natural-born sharpshooter, but that is very rare. Some of the best shots in the army are men who, at the start, hardly knew how to handle firearms."

At this target practice a perfect score would have netted twenty-five points. The contest went on merrily, and at the conclusion it was found that Andy had scored ten points; Randy, twelve; Jack, eighteen; and Fred, nineteen. One other cadet, a youth named Lewis Barrow, had scored twenty.

"Well, the prize goes to Barrow!" cried Jack.

"Yes. But we came pretty close to winning," cried Fred, with justifiable pride.

"You and Jack needn't complain," was Andy's comment. "Eighteen and nineteen points out of a possible twenty-five is going some, especially for beginners."

"If I win the prize, what is it?" questioned Lewis Barrow, a tall, lanky youth with a rather leathery face. He came from the far West, and knew much more about firearms than did the Rovers.

"Oh, the prize is first choice of holes in half a dozen doughnuts," snickered Andy.

"Holes in doughnuts!" replied Barrow, who was not over-bright. "Suffering buffaloes! What would a fellow do with holes out of doughnuts?" and at this there was a little laugh.

"For beginners, I think you have all done very well," remarked Captain Dale. "The lowest score, I see, is nine. Last year when the new cadets went at practice, we had several fellows who didn't hit the target."

"Gee! I'd hate to go hunting with such chaps," was Andy's dry comment. "A fellow would have to get right directly in front of 'em to be sure of not being hit;" and this remark made even the military instructor laugh.

"I'll be proud of all of you," said Major Ralph Mason, when he heard of the scores that had been made. "First thing you know, we'll have a company of genuine sharpshooters."

"This practising at a target will come in fine if we get a chance to do any hunting this winter," remarked Fred. "Wow! Just think what would have happened if that target had been a deer, or even a partridge!"

"A deer or a partridge isn't apt to stand still," returned Randy. "If you want to become expert as a hunting shot, you'll have to practise at a swinging target."

"Well, that's to come later, so Captain Dale said," was the answer.

Arthur M. Winfield

"Say, let's go out hunting some day when the season opens!" cried Jack. "I'd like first rate to bag something, even if it were only a few rabbits."

"That's the talk!" answered Fred, quickly. "As soon as the hunting season opens let's go out, by all means."

The target practice had been witnessed by Slugger Brown and Nappy Martell. Now, when Jack and Fred spoke of hunting, Slugger Brown's face became thoughtful.

"I think I see a way to square accounts with those Rovers," he remarked to his crony. "From now on, I'm going to watch 'em pretty closely. If ever they do go out hunting, I think we'll be able to put one over on 'em they'll never forget."

CHAPTER XXIV

THE FUN OF HALLOWE'EN

"Hallowe'en to-morrow night, boys! So get ready for some real fun!"

"Right you are, Andy! Remember what fun we had last year in New York?"

"And what fun we had down on the farm two years ago, scaring Aleck Pop and Jack Ness nearly to death?" broke in Fred.

"I don't know whether they'll let us have any fun around Colby Hall or not," remarked Jack, but in such a tone of voice that all of the others knew he was fooling.

Several days had passed since the target practice, and the boys were gathered in the room used by Andy and Randy for studying. All were deep in a discussion of what they might do on Hallowe'en, when there came a knock on the door and Dan Soppinger came in.

"Excuse me for interrupting you," commenced Dan, "but I'm up against a hard proposition. Can any of you tell me—"

Arthur M. Winfield

"Gee! the Human Question Mark is at it again!" broke out Randy.

"Certainly we can tell you," put in Andy; "but please don't ask it."

"Three and three make six, three and three always have made six, and three and three always will make six!" cried Fred in a girlish tone of voice. "So what's the use of asking a question like that?"

"Who said anything about three and three making six?" snorted the Human Question Mark. "What I was going to say was: Can any of you tell me—"

"When Nero discovered the north pole?" interrupted Andy.

"No. He wants to know when Washington first crossed the Pacific in a motor boat," came from Fred.

"No; that isn't it at all," declared Jack, seriously. "Dan wants to know what kind of an automobile Noah took on the ark."

"Great Scott! What do you take me for?" groaned Dan Soppinger, helplessly. "Here I come in to ask you a perfectly simple question, and you start with a lot of foolishness."

"Why, my dear Dan, we are helping you all we can!" cried Andy in deeply injured tones.

"I want to know when Florida was first settled and by whom!" cried Dan, desperately. "I bet ten cents none of you know!"

"Oh, that's easy, Dan," answered Andy, gravely. "Florida was first settled by the alligators, in the year one;" and at this remark there was such a burst of laughter that the Human Question Mark gave it up in despair and fled.

"I've got a great scheme for Hallowe'en," said Andy a little later. He had been walking up and down the room trying to make up his mind what they might do to have some fun. "I wonder if the girls over at Clearwater Hall wouldn't lend us some dresses and some girls' hats for the occasion."

"They might if we agreed to lend them some of our suits in exchange."

"Well, we could do that easily enough," answered Fred. "We hardly ever have a chance to wear anything these days but our uniforms."

"What do you want to do, Andy—dress up as a girl?" questioned Jack.

"That's it. We might have dead loads of fun."

The matter was discussed for a time, and in the end a boy, who often did errands for the cadets, was dispatched to Clearwater Hall with a note to Ruth and her chums. The boy had performed this sort of service before, and knew that he must deliver the note without allowing the communication to go through the school office.

The messenger returned just as the cadets were on the point of retiring, and brought back a letter from the girls in which they agreed to let the boys have what they wanted in return for some suits of male attire. It was agreed that the exchange be made in the afternoon, directly after the school session.

The Rover boys and two of their friends walked to Haven Point, and there invested some of their spending money in

Arthur M. Winfield

the hire of an automobile. Then they rode back to the school, procured several bundles of clothing, and set out for Clearwater Hall.

The girls were waiting for them at a spot secluded from observation, and there an exchange of bundles took place, interspersed with a good deal of laughing by the cadets and giggling on the part of the Clearwater pupils.

"Oh, I'd love to see you dressed up as a girl!" cried Ruth to Jack.

"How about your being dressed up as a boy?" he returned.

"Oh, none of us will dare show ourselves outside the grounds," returned Ruth, blushing. "Miss Garwood wouldn't permit it."

"Well, if we get the chance, we may come up as far as yonder side fence," put in Fred. "If we do, we'll give you the signal—three long whistles."

Nearly all of the cadets at Colby Hall were ready for Hallowe'en fun. They dressed up in all sorts of disguises, including those of monks, Indians, negroes, and ghosts. Lighted pumpkins with grinning faces cut into them were likewise numerous; and one senior trailed around in a silk gown which he had brought from home for this very occasion.

When the Rover boys appeared dressed as young ladies, with girls' hats on their heads and parasols in their hands, they were greeted with a loud cheer, and this was redoubled as they marched around the campus arm in arm with several boys dressed as dudes, and one attired as an admiral.

"Some class to the Rovers, and no mistake!" was Spouter's

comment. He had on a pair of long whiskers, a linen duster, farm boots, and a big straw hat.

"How do you do, Uncle Si?" cried Andy, coming up to him and bowing. "How is corn?"

"So high, by gosh! y'u can't see the house," answered Spouter in country dialect. "Do tell, leetle gal! but y'u do look mighty purty, y'u do!" and at this there was a general snicker.

At the first opportunity, the Rovers and several of their friends slipped away from the campus and hurried off in the direction of Clearwater Hall. They were lucky enough to meet a big wagon, the driver of which was going to the next town to pick up some young folks for a straw ride. This man took them to the young ladies' school just for the sport of it.

When the Rovers gave the signal, Ruth and her friends came running towards the side fence of the grounds. All were attired in male costumes, wearing exaggerated collars, cuffs and neckties. In addition, Ruth had on a big pair of pick-toed shoes and a silk hat many years out of date. She also carried a silver-headed cane.

"Oh, don't you want to take us out for a walk?" questioned Andy, in a high-pitched, feminine voice.

"Very sorry, my dear, very sorry," came from May Powell, in as deep a voice as she could command. "I have important business to attend to."

"Oh, Jack, what an awfully big girl you do make!" screamed Ruth, when she discovered his identity behind the little mask he wore. "I didn't know you were so large."

Arthur M. Winfield

"And what a little man you are," he answered, gaily.

"Don't say a word," she returned. "See these sleeves? They are all rolled up; and I had to do the same with the trousers," and she laughed merrily.

Although acting against the rules, the Rovers and their friends found an opening in the fence, and for a brief quarter of an hour mingled with the girls on the campus of the school. They had "a barrel of fun," to use Andy's way of expressing it, and left only because it was getting late and they knew they would have to walk all the way back to Colby Hall.

"This is about the best Hallowe'en fun we ever had," remarked Jack, while he and the others were on the return to the school.

To make time, the boys did not take the regular road through Haven Point to Colby Hall, but tramped along a back highway which was considered something of a short cut. This presently brought them in sight of a large farm which belonged to a hard-fisted man named Elias Lacy.

"Say, we ought to call on old Lacy and give him a scare," said Randy, coming to a halt near the farmhouse.

"It would serve him right!" answered Fred, promptly.

None of the Rovers had a kindly feeling for Elias Lacy, for the reason that the old man had once caught them getting chestnuts from a tree on the corner of his farm and had made them give up all the nuts they had gathered and had then threatened them with the law if they dared to set foot on his premises again.

"I know you cadets," he had snarled. "You are all a pack of petty thieves! I want you to keep away from here."

He had suffered a great deal, some cadets, including Slugger Brown and Nappy Martell, having at various times robbed him of his cherries, his strawberries, and some melons. Of these depredations, however, the Rovers knew nothing.

"Maybe Lacy isn't around," remarked Jack. "He may have gone to town."

They knew that the old man was a bachelor. He had two young men working for him, and also a woman who came in during the day to do the housework, but all of these went home at night.

"I see somebody moving around the house now," answered Randy. "It's Lacy, too!"

"Let's knock on the door and pretend we are young ladies in distress," cried Randy. "Come on! I wonder what he'll do?"

"Don't ask him for any money. He won't give you a cent," chuckled Fred.

"Let's tell him some tramps stopped us and that we want him to go out and fight the fellows," suggested one cadet. "That will show how brave a man Lacy is. We can take off our masks."

So it was arranged, and in a minute more the boys were all on the front piazza of the farmhouse ringing the old doorbell. There was a sound within, and in a moment more Elias Lacy came to the door with a lamp in one hand.

"What do you want?" he asked in astonishment, when he saw

what looked to be a number of well-dressed girls confronting him.

"Oh, Mr. Lacy, won't you please protect us?" pleaded Randy, in his best feminine voice.

"Three murderous tramps are after us!" gasped Andy. "Oh, dear! I know I shall faint!"

"The tramps wanted to rob us!" cried Jack.

"They are just outside your fence," put in Fred. "Please go out and chase them away."

Elias Lacy was staggered. He placed his lamp on a little table near by, and looked in wonder at the crowd before him.

"Three tramps, eh? An' goin' to rob you? Why, I never heard of sech a thing!" he shrilled. "Mebbe I'd better git my gun."

"Oh, yes! yes! Get your gun, by all means! Get your gun! And maybe you'd better get a sword, too!" cried Randy.

"Yes! Or a knife or a—a—razor," put in Andy.

"Now, now! don't git so excited!" cried the old man, for the boys insisted upon clinging to his arms and to his shoulders. "Them tramps ain't goin' to eat you up."

He was short-sighted, and, as the lamplight was poor, he had not noticed the boys' somewhat crude make-up. He hurried into a room and came forth presently carrying a shotgun. Then he walked back into his kitchen.

"Great Caesar! he's got his gun all right enough," said Jack in a low voice.

"Maybe he'll use it on us when he discovers the trick," returned Fred.

"I'll git my lantern, an' then we kin go after them tramps," announced Elias Lacy; and in a moment more he reappeared with a smoky lantern and started for the front door. "Come on, an' show me where them tramps are," he said, determinedly.

Arthur M. Winfield

CHAPTER XXV

OFF ON A HUNT

"Say, as soon as we are outdoors let us give him the ha-ha and run away," whispered Fred to the others.

"Oh, no! Let's have some more fun," pleaded Randy. "Why! the sport has just begun!"

"That's it!" came from his twin.

"Don't forget we are due at the Hall," remonstrated Jack.

"Now then, show me them tramps!" cried Elias Lacy, as the whole crowd went outdoors and towards the front gate.

"Oh, protect us! Please protect us!" shrieked Randy, and caught hold of the old man's coat-tails.

"Don't let the tramps abduct us! I don't want to live with any tramp! I want to marry a millionaire!" screamed Andy, and began to cling so close to Elias Lacy that the old man could hardly move forward.

The twins cut up so that the others had all they could do to keep from laughing. One boy began to snicker, but promptly clapped his hand over his mouth.

"Don't hang on to me," ordered the old farmer. "I can't use my gun if you clutch my arm like that," and he tried to shake the twins off.

"Oh, there they are—behind the bushes!" screamed Randy, suddenly, pointing off to the left.

"Where?" demanded the old man, holding his lantern over his head. "I don't see nothin'."

"There they are!" screamed Andy. "They've got pistols, too! Oh, save us! Save us!"

"Drat the pesky rascals! I'll fix 'em!" snarled Elias Lacy, and, shaking loose the clinging boys, he ran off, lantern in one hand and shotgun held up to his shoulder with the other.

"Now is our time to skip out!" cried Jack.

"Right you are!" added another of the crowd. And then without waiting for the rest, this cadet let up a cry: "Sold! Mr. Lacy, you are sold!"

"Sold! With the compliments of the Colby Hall cadets!" cried another. And then, seeing that the disguise was at an end, the boys began to shout a variety of things not at all complimentary to the old farmer.

Elias Lacy was thunderstruck by the sudden turn of affairs, and, wheeling around, he stared in open-mouthed wonder at the retreating girlish figures.

"What's that?" he shrilled. "What are you runnin' away fur?"

Arthur M. Winfield

"Good-bye, Mr. Lacy!" sang out Randy. "We're only having a little fun."

"Don't you know it's Hallowe'en?" queried Andy; and then started to walk off on his hands, but the dress he wore fell down around him and caused him to tumble over on his back. In the gloom, Fred stumbled and fell on top of him.

"Fun! Hallowe'en!" bellowed Elias Lacy, and of a sudden he became filled with rage. "You ain't gals at all! You're only playin' a trick on me!" he snarled.

"Good-bye and pleasant dreams!" shouted Randy.

"Don't tell any of your friends about the young ladies who called on you," advised Jack.

And then the other cadets made various taunting remarks. They had come to a halt to enjoy the old farmer's discomfiture and at the same time to give Andy and Fred a chance to regain their feet.

"Halt!" suddenly commanded Elias Lacy, and set down his lantern on a fence post. "Halt! or I'll shoot some of you!" and he aimed his shotgun at them.

"Don't shoot!" cried several of the cadets in alarm, for they could see that the old man was in a frame of mind to do almost anything.

"Stop! Don't you dare stir a step or I'll shoot as sure as you're standin' there!" continued the old man. And then, as all of the boys halted he went on: "Now come up here where I kin git a good look at you, but don't you come too clost or try to play any more tricks. If you do, somebody'll sure git shot."

There was no help for it, and rather sheepishly the crowd of cadets came forward as he had ordered.

"It was only a bit of Hallowe'en fun. We didn't mean any harm," pleaded Randy.

"Take them bunnets an' things off so I kin see your faces," ordered the old man, at the same time keeping the crowd covered with his shotgun.

With great reluctance one after another the cadets took off their veils and hats. The old man came a step or two closer, looking at each face sharply. His countenance grew even more hateful when he recognized the Rovers.

"Ha! you're the same fellers who robbed my chestnut tree," he snarled. "Didn't I tell you to keep off my premises? I've a good mind to have you locked up."

"Oh, come, Mr. Lacy, it was only a bit of fun," pleaded one lad. "Didn't you go out on Hallowe'ens when you were a boy?"

"No, I didn't! I stayed home an' done my work," was the harsh reply. "Nowadays boys cut up altogether too much."

Had it not been for the shotgun the boys would have taken to their heels; but with the old man thus armed none of them wanted to take any chances. But then came a lucky interruption. From back on the farm came a wild bellowing as if a cow was in trouble. This was followed by the squealing of a number of pigs.

"Hello! Those town boys must have come over after your cattle after all!" cried Jack, struck by a sudden idea.

Arthur M. Winfield

"My cattle! What do you know about my cattle?" questioned Elias Lacy, quickly.

"That's it! The town boys are after the cows and pigs!" broke in Fred, quick to catch Jack's idea.

"You'll lose them all if you don't look out, Mr. Lacy!" put in Randy.

"They sha'n't tech my cows, nor my pigs neither!" snarled the old farmer; and, taking up his lantern, he left the cadets and ran off towards the rear of the premises. Fortunately, nothing serious had happened to his stock.

"Now's the time to skip out!" cried Jack, and led the way, and the others lost no time in following. The cadets had to hold their skirts high to keep from tripping as they sped along. They reached Colby Hall in safety, and lost no time in rejoining their friends. A little later the Hallowe'en celebration came to an end.

"Old Lacy will remember us," was Andy's comment, in speaking of the affair the next day. "He'll have it in for us."

"I'm afraid so," replied Jack, seriously.

The main topic of conversation at the school now was the football game which was to take place with the eleven of the Clearwater Country Club on the following Saturday. This was another gala occasion for the school, and once more the boys had the pleasure of escorting the girls to and from the conflict.

"I hope we can do them up as we did Hixley High," remarked Jack. But this was not to be. The Clearwater Country Club eleven were much older than the cadets and much heavier, and all the Colby Hall team could do was to hold them down to a score of 16 to 10.

"Well, that's not so bad but what it might be worse," remarked Gif, when the defeated eleven had returned to Colby Hall. "I did hope, however, that we might hold them to at least a tie."

"They carried too much weight for us," replied Jack. "Even Slugger Brown couldn't do anything against them." For Slugger had been used as a substitute in the third and fourth quarters. But the big cadet had failed to show either form or efficiency. He had been warned by the umpire, because of an unfair tackle, and this had put him in anything but a good humor.

"I won't play again so long as Gif Garrison is captain!" cried Slugger to Nappy Martell; and that evening he sent in his resignation, which Gif promptly accepted.

The game with Columbus Academy was not to take place until two weeks later, so that, although they kept at their practice, the football players had considerable time for other things. Jack and his cousins had continued their target practice, and their shooting was now so accurate that Captain Dale complimented them upon it.

"The hunting season opens to-morrow," announced Jack one day, as he came back from an errand to the town. "How I'd like to go out and try my luck!"

"I'd like to go myself," spoke up Fred.

A number of the senior cadets had received permission to go hunting and Jack spoke to one of these youths about the prospects.

"I'd like first rate to have you come with me, Rover," said the cadet, Frank Newberry by name; "and if your cousin Fred wants to come along, he can do so."

"We'd have to get permission first, and also permission to use a couple of the shotguns," answered Jack. The gun rack at Colby Hall boasted a number of these weapons, but none of them could be taken out and used without special permission from Captain Dale.

It was no easy matter for Jack and Fred to gain the desired permission, but when Colonel Colby heard from Captain Dale what good shots the boys had proved to be, he said they might go out, along with Frank Newberry and some of the others.

"But I want you to be very careful," said the colonel impressively. "I wouldn't have an accident happen to you for the world. Don't fire a charge until you are absolutely sure of what you're firing at. Never point your gun at anybody else; and be very careful how you handle your weapon in climbing a fence or leaping over rocks or brushwood."

The twins were a bit envious over the prospects for their cousins, but they wished Jack and Fred the best of luck. All of the cadets who were to go out had lessons in the morning, but they departed directly after dinner, and were told that they could remain out as long as they pleased.

"Now, don't forget to bring back a deer or a bear," cried Andy.

"And if you can, bag a buffalo or a hippopotamus," added his twin.

"We'll be lucky if we bag some rabbits and a squirrel or two or some woodcock," answered Jack. "Big game doesn't exist around here any more. The farms are too thick."

"Well, be sure and bring down a pink canary bird, anyway," advised Andy; and at this there was a general laugh.

Frank Newberry had been out the year before, and consequently knew much about the lay of the land.

"We'll go down into the woods directly back of Haven Point," he announced. "Last year the hunting there was much better than it was up the Rick Rack River."

And then off the cadets started on the hunt. Much that was unusual lay in store for them.

　　　　　Arthur M. Winfield

CHAPTER XXVI

FROM ONE TROUBLE TO ANOTHER

Half an hour of tramping brought the two Rover boys and their friends into the heart of the big woods Frank Newberry had mentioned. They had entered it by way of the road they had used on Hallowe'en, and were now almost directly behind Elias Lacy's farm. In fact, although they were not aware of this, a large section of the woods belonged to the old farmer.

On their way into the timber they had heard various shots at a distance, showing that other hunters were abroad. Then came a report so close at hand, it made Fred jump.

"You want to be very careful so that you don't mistake some other hunter for game," cautioned Frank Newberry.

"Exactly!" grumbled Fred. "And I want the other hunters to be careful that they don't shoot me for a deer or a bear."

The cadets continued to advance into the woods, and then crossed an open space. Here they were fortunate enough to stir up quite a few rabbits, and Jack, after an hour's hunt, had the pleasure of bringing down two, while one was laid low by Fred.

So far the cadets had kept together, but presently the party managed to catch sight of game in two directions, and soon Frank Newberry and the seniors with him were hurrying off to the southward while the Rover boys went after game that had gone northward.

"Come right back to this spot!" cried Frank Newberry to the Rovers.

"All right," answered Jack.

Their sporting blood, aroused by the game already brought down, urged Jack and Fred forward, and almost before they knew it they had covered a long distance. They presently came to another clearing, bordering a good-sized pond. Here they stirred up half a dozen rabbits and also some squirrels, and each succeeded in bringing down more than half the game sighted.

"Say, this is the finest sport ever!" declared Fred, as he looked at his game with deep satisfaction. "Won't the others envy us when we get back to the Hall with these!"

"It's sport enough for us," returned Jack. "I don't know what the rabbits and squirrels think about it though," he added dryly.

From a distance the boys had seen more game and they began to circle the pond. Then they heard a strange whirring in some bushes a distance further on.

"Maybe we'll come across some wild turkeys or something like that," said Fred.

"I don't believe there are any wild turkeys around here," answered Jack.

Arthur M. Winfield

"Oh! wouldn't it be fine if we sighted a deer or a bear?" sighed Fred.

"You don't want much for your money, do you?" laughed his cousin. "I rather think if a bear came after you you'd take to your heels."

"Maybe I would—if he was a big one."

On and on went the two boys, and presently were rewarded by the sight of several small woodcock. Both fired almost at the same instant, and two of the birds came fluttering down, to thrash around in the bushes until put out of misery by the young hunters.

"Two of 'em! Think of that!" chuckled Fred. "Oh! this is simply glorious!"

So far the two boys had not met any of the strange hunters, but now they came across two men well loaded down with rabbits. They did not know it, but one of the men was a farm hand employed by Elias Lacy.

"You'd better keep away from the Lacy place," said the man, with a sarcastic look at the Rovers. He had been on hand when the lads had had the chestnuts taken away by the old farmer, and had also heard about the joke on Hallowe'en.

"Don't you worry. We've no use for Mr. Lacy," returned Fred, crossly.

"He's the meanest man we ever met," added Jack. At this the farm hand only grinned, and then he and his companion disappeared once more into the woods.

So far the day had been typical of the Autumn season,

somewhat gray, with only an occasional showing of the sun. Now, however, it became rapidly darker, and presently a few flakes of snow sifted down through the air.

"Hello! What do you know about this!" cried Jack, looking up. "I guess we're going to have a snowstorm."

"Oh, I hope it doesn't snow very heavily—at least not until we get back to school," returned Fred, quickly.

"A little snow won't hurt us, Fred."

"But if it got too thick, Jack, we might lose our way."

"I don't believe it will come down as heavily as all that—not at this season of the year."

With the sky growing darker, and the flakes of snow coming down thicker than ever, the two boys sought to retrace their steps in the direction of the pond. But in their eagerness to sight something at which to shoot, they had not noted their path very carefully, and as a consequence they now found themselves somewhat bewildered.

"If the sun was only out we'd know in what direction to steer," remarked Jack. "But when the sky is this way, a fellow is apt to get completely turned around."

"It's too bad we didn't bring a pocket compass."

"That's true. However, we haven't got one, so we'll have to make the best of it. Come on!"

They had paused for a moment to rest and to survey their surroundings. Now they continued their tramping, and at length came out on the edge of a sheet of water which they at first took to be the pond they had previously visited.

"There they go! Quick, Jack!" sang out Fred, and blazed away with his shotgun. His cousin followed suit, and soon they found they had bagged two additional rabbits—one the largest yet brought low.

"This isn't the pond at all!" cried Jack, in some disappointment, after the excitement of shooting the rabbits had subsided. "I never saw this spot before."

"Nor I! What do you make of it, Jack?"

"Don't ask me! It looks as if we were lost."

"Hark! I heard a shot!" cried Fred, a minute later, while the pair were looking around trying to make up their minds in what direction to proceed next. "Maybe those are our fellows shooting."

The shot had come from their right, and was presently followed by another. Thinking their friends might be close at hand, the Rovers started off as well as they could through the brushwood and between the trees. But then they came to some rough ground covered with rocks, and here further progress was all but impossible. In the meanwhile, no further reports had reached their ears.

"We are sure up against it," remarked Jack, after he and his cousin had looked at each other rather helplessly. It was darker than ever, and the snow still continued to sift down through the trees.

"Maybe we'll have to stay out here all night," said Fred, after consulting his watch. "It's half past five now."

"We ought to be on the way back to the Hall if we expect any supper," replied his cousin.

Being unable to advance further in that direction, the Rover boys sought to retrace their steps, and after considerable trouble managed to return to the sheet of water they had left a while before. But by this time the darkness of night had fallen.

"It's no use!" cried Fred, helplessly. "We're lost, that's all there is to it!"

"It was bad enough while it was daylight, Fred. I really don't know what we are going to do now it's dark," answered Jack, seriously.

On the return to the little pond Fred had stumbled over some tree roots, and this had lamed him a little.

"I can't walk very much further," he said, with a sigh. And then he added quickly: "Jack, have you any matches?"

"Oh, yes! I put a box in my pocket before we started."

"Good! Then if we have to stay here we can build a fire and maybe cook something."

The boys tried the water of the pond, and finding it fairly good drank their fill. Then they sat down to discuss the situation. Both were hungry, and in the end they gathered some dry sticks, started a fire, and cooked one of the rabbits and also a squirrel, which they ate with much satisfaction.

"We'll freeze to death if we stay here all night," was Fred's dismal comment.

Arthur M. Winfield

"Oh, no—not if we keep the fire going."

"Then let's do that by all means. It will not only keep us warm, but it may be the means of directing somebody to this place."

It was a long night for both of the boys. They took turns at resting and at replenishing the fire, and it is doubtful if either of them got much real sleep. Once, in the early morning, came an alarm, and Fred imagined a bear was in the bushes. But the animal, or whatever it was, soon went away, and that was the end of the disturbance.

"Thank goodness! it has stopped snowing!" remarked Jack, when the cousins were preparing a breakfast of another squirrel.

The snow had not amounted to much, being less than an inch in depth. The storm had cleared away entirely, and at the proper time the sun came up over the hills beyond Clearwater Lake.

Long before that time the two young hunters were once more on their way. They had tramped along for fully half an hour when suddenly Jack let up a shout of joy.

"Hurrah! we've struck a road at last! Now we'll find out where we are!"

The road was little more than a trail through the woods, evidently made by the wagon or sled of some woodcutter. It ran down a slight hill, and the two boys lost no time in following it.

"I hope it brings us into Haven Point," remarked Fred, as they strode along. "I'm getting tired of walking and of carrying the shotgun. I'd rather have a ride."

"Let us be thankful to get out of the woods, Fred. We might have gotten so mixed up that we'd have had to spend another night there."

The two lads continued to follow the woods road, and presently came into sight of several farm buildings, including a corncrib and a long, low cowshed.

"Oh, for the love of doughnuts!" cried Jack an instant later. "Fred, do you know where we are?"

"No, I don't. Where?"

"Right in the back of old Lacy's place! There is his house;" and the oldest Rover boy pointed with his hand.

"You're right, Jack! Gee! we almost ran into the old man again, didn't we?" gasped Fred. "We had better get out of here as quick as we can!"

"Now you're saying something!" returned his cousin. "Come on, before he catches sight of us!"

The two boys had just started to leave the road on which they had been traveling when a shout reached their ears. The next moment another shout rent the frosty morning air, and then two men came running towards the lads, one carrying a gun and the other a pitchfork.

"Stop there! you young rascals! Stop!" roared out the voice of Elias Lacy. "Stop, I tell you! Caleb, cover 'em with your gun!"

"I'm doin' it, Mr. Lacy," replied the other man, and leveled

Arthur M. Winfield

his gun at the boys. He was the same man the Rovers had met in the woods the afternoon before.

With the weapon of the farm hand pointed at them the two Rover boys came to a halt. In a minute more the others came up, Elias Lacy puffing because of his exertions.

"Now I've caught you!" he snarled. "I didn't think it was goin' to be so easy."

"You're certainly in luck, Mr. Lacy," grinned Caleb Boggs. "I didn't think they'd stay roun' here after doin' it."

"They came back jest to have the laugh on me!" snarled the old farmer. "I know 'em! I s'pose they did it 'cause I took them chestnuts away from 'em, an' on account o' the way I treated 'em Hallowe'en night. But I'll fix 'em now! I'll have the law on 'em! I'll send 'em to state's prison for ten years! Jest you see if I don't!" and thus the old man spluttered on, saying many things the boys could not understand.

"See here, Mr. Lacy! What are you so mad about?" queried Jack, finally. "Can't you stand a little fun?"

"Stand a little fun!" yelled the excited old man, fairly beside himself with rage. "It ain't no fun to kill two o' my cows!" He shook his bony fist at the boys. "I'll have the law on you, so I will! I'll send you both to state's prison for ten years!"

CHAPTER XXVII

ELIAS LACY'S DEMAND

The two Rover boys stared at Elias Lacy in open-mouthed amazement.

"What did you say about killing two cows?" questioned Jack.

"Have two of your cows been killed?" came from Fred.

At these questions the old farmer seemed to become more enraged than ever. He raised his pitchfork as if to use it on the cadets.

"You can't play innercent with me!" he fairly screamed. "I know you! You shot them cows, an' I'm a-goin' to send you to state's prison fur it!"

"It's a purty serious business—killin' a man's cattle like that," added Caleb Boggs, with a shake of his head. He still held his shotgun so as to cover the two boys.

"I don't know a thing about your cows, and I certainly haven't shot at them," answered Jack, indignantly.

"We haven't been anywhere near your cow pasture, or your

Arthur M. Winfield

cowshed, either," said Fred. "We've been hunting up in the woods yonder. Your man saw us."

"We got lost up there after it began to snow, and we had to camp out all night," explained Jack. "We just found that road and were trying to get back to Haven Point and Colby Hall."

"It ain't so! It ain't so!" snarled Elias Lacy. "You come over to my cow paster yesterday afternoon an' shot both o' them cows and then you run away. One o' my men seen you."

"He never did!" burst out Jack. "I tell you we weren't near your place."

"We went out hunting with a number of other cadets, and we can prove it!" added his cousin.

"Huh! where are them other cadets now?" demanded the old farmer.

"We got separated in the woods—they going off for some rabbits in one direction and we going off after some other rabbits in another direction," explained the oldest Rover boy. "I don't know where those other cadets are now. Probably they went back to the school."

"You ain't got no right to hunt on my grounds."

"We were out in the open woods, Mr. Lacy, where we had a perfect right to be."

"Well, we won't talk about that now," snarled the old man. "I'm a-goin' to fix you for shootin' them cows. They was two of the best cows I had, an' they was wuth a lot o' money."

A wordy war followed, during which the boys became

almost as angry as the old farmer. They insisted upon it that they had not been near his farm during the afternoon of the day before, but he did not believe a word they said.

"I'm a-goin' to have the law on you!" he cried. "I'm a-goin' to have you arrested! An' I'll make your folks pay fur them cows!"

"Hadn't we better march 'em down to the barn?" suggested the hired man. "Then I kin hitch up the horses and we kin take 'em down to the town lock-up."

"Oh, Jack, don't let them lock us up!" whispered Fred, in horror.

"If you lock us up, Mr. Lacy, you'll suffer for it," said Jack. "I'll get my father to sue you for damages."

"Don't you talk to me like that, you young whipper-snapper!" cried the old man. "I know what I'm a-doin'. I'm a-goin' to turn you over to the town authorities, an' that's all there is to it!"

The old man was obdurate, and he and the hired man forced the boys into the barn, where the farmer stood guard with the shotgun while the hired man hooked up a team of horses to one of the farm wagons. Then the lads were told to get into the turnout.

"I don't think I'll get in," said Jack.

"Yes, you will!" snarled Elias Lacy; and then followed a lively scuffle. But the two boys were no match for the men, and they were quickly disarmed. Then, being covered by the hired man's shotgun, they had to get up into the wagon. The hired man drove, while Elias Lacy sat in the rear, the shotgun ready for action so that the boys might not escape. Their own

Arthur M. Winfield

guns, along with their game, were placed on the bottom of the wagon under a blanket.

It must be confessed that Jack and Fred were in no enviable frame of mind as the wagon with the two prisoners aboard headed in the direction of Haven Point. They knew that news of their arrest would spread rapidly, and they wondered what their friends, and especially the girls at Clearwater Hall, would think of it.

"Gee, but we're in a pickle!" commented Fred, dismally.

"Yes. And the worst of it is, I don't know how we are going to clear ourselves," answered his cousin. "As near as I can learn, those cows were shot while you and I were off by ourselves in the woods. The hired man says the other man who works on the place saw two cadets disappearing between the trees."

"Who can those fellows be, Jack?"

"Don't ask me! Probably two of our fellows who have some grudge against Lacy."

This talk was carried on in an undertone, so that neither the old farmer nor his hired man could understand what was said.

"You needn't plan no trick to escape," warned Elias Lacy, raising his shotgun slightly.

"Mr. Lacy, what did you do with the two cows that were shot?" asked Jack, suddenly.

"I left 'em out in the paster, right where they fell," returned the old farmer. "I ain't a-goin' to tech 'em till the authorities have looked 'em over."

"Were they killed with bird shot or with rifle bullets?"

"Bird shot—same as you've been a-usin' in them shotguns of yourn."

A portion of the roadway leading into Haven Point was being repaired and was closed off; so, in order to get down into the town, they had to make something of a detour in the direction of Colby Hall.

"Oh, Jack, hadn't we better ask him to take us to the Hall first?" whispered Fred to his cousin. "Maybe Colonel Colby can fix this up for us."

"I might ask him," returned Jack, in a low tone.

"I ain't a-goin' to Colby Hall," snarled Elias Lacy, after the question had been put to him. "I'm a-goin' to take you to the lock-up."

The journey towards the town was continued, and presently those in the wagon came within sight of a rural free delivery turnout.

"Hello there, Pete! Got any letters for us?" sang out the farm hand.

"One fur Mr. Lacy," replied the post carrier, and, driving closer, he handed it over.

"I ain't got no time to read letters now," announced Elias Lacy, as he thrust the communication into his pocket. "I've got other business to 'tend to."

"Givin' a couple of the Colby cadets a ride, eh?" ventured the carrier.

"I'm a-takin' 'em to the lock-up, Pete. They went an' shot two o' my cows."

"You don't say, 'Lias!" cried the carrier in amazement. "Out huntin' I s'pose, and mistook 'em for deer or bears," and he chuckled over his little joke.

"No; they done it a-purpose," growled the farmer. "They held a grudge agin me, an' they thought they was a-goin' to git square. But I'll show 'em, an' don't you forgit it!"

"We didn't shoot his cows!" came simultaneously from Jack and Fred.

"Bad business! But I've got to be on my way," commented the carrier. "That road bein' closed puts me away off my regular route;" and off he drove.

Three quarters of the distance to Haven Point had been covered when those in the wagon heard a shout, and a moment later Captain Dale came galloping up on horseback.

"Where in the world have you two cadets been?" he cried. "We have been looking all over for you."

"We got lost in the woods and had to camp out all night," explained Jack, and then added: "Did the others get back?"

"Oh, yes. And they fully expected that you would follow them." And then, seeing a peculiar look on the boys' faces, the military instructor of Colby Hall continued: "Nothing wrong, I hope?"

"Yes, there is—a whole lot wrong!" cried Elias Lacy, before the cadets could answer. "They sneaked up to my farm an' shot two o' my cows."

"Impossible!" exclaimed the military man.

"No, it ain't! It's so!" shrilled the old farmer. "They killed the cows, an' I'm on my way to put 'em in the Haven Point lock-up."

"Oh, Captain Dale, don't let him have us arrested!" pleaded Fred. "We do not know anything about his cows, and we certainly did not shoot them."

"Tell me all about this," demanded Captain Dale. And in a highly excited fashion, Elias Lacy told his story, which was corroborated by his hired man.

"Now I'll hear what you have to say," said the captain, turning to Jack and Fred.

They gave him the particulars of what had happened, just as they had already related them to the old farmer. Then Captain Dale asked them a number of questions. Elias Lacy interrupted continually.

"I ain't a-goin' to stand no nonsense," said the old man doggedly. "I'm a-goin' to put 'em in the lock-up, an' do it right now!"

"Mr. Lacy, allow me to tell you something," said the military instructor coolly. "If these boys are guilty you will be justified in having them placed under arrest. But if they are not guilty—and they claim they are innocent—you'll make yourself liable for a big suit for damages."

Arthur M. Winfield

"I don't care! I know they shot them cows!"

"No, you don't know it. You admit that the farm hand who saw the two cadets did not recognize them. In fact, he wasn't altogether sure that they were cadets. Now, these boys claim they were nowhere near your pasture lot when the cows were shot. I think the best thing you can do is to let them return to the Hall with me. Colonel Colby is away to-day, but I will take the matter up with him just as soon as he returns."

"Mebbe if I let 'em go to the Hall, they'll run away," answered Elias Lacy. The mention of a possible lawsuit for damages had taken some of the aggressiveness out of him.

"I will see to it that they do not run away," answered Captain Dale. "We have a guardroom at the Hall—a sort of lock-up; and if it is necessary I will have them placed there until Colonel Colby can investigate, and until you can make up your mind what you want to do."

The old farmer argued the matter for several minutes, but in the end agreed to let the military instructor take charge of Jack and Fred.

"But remember," he said in parting, "you've got to keep 'em under lock an' key till I see Colonel Colby. I'm a-goin' to make an investigation, an' I'm purty sure I'll be able to prove that they killed them cows."

CHAPTER XXVIII

IN THE GUARDROOM

"What in the world do you suppose has become of them, Randy?"

"I give it up! I hope they only lost their way and didn't have some kind of an accident."

"Oh, don't speak of an accident!" cried Andy in horror. "It makes me shiver to think of it."

"I can't understand why they didn't rejoin us as they promised to do," said Frank Newberry, who was present. "We looked all over for them, and fired one or two shots to attract their attention, but it was all useless."

The twins had passed a restless night following the continued absence from the school of their cousins. Early in the morning they had gone out in company with Gif and Spouter, and covered many miles in a vain search for the absent ones. They could not settle down to their class work, and so were excused by Professor Brice.

"Well, I've got to be getting back to the classroom," remarked Frank Newberry, presently, and he and several others who were present hurried away, leaving the twins to themselves.

The boys walked down the roadway which had been followed by the hunters the day before. They had covered only a short distance when they saw a farm wagon approaching, with Captain Dale beside it on his horse.

"There they are!" cried Andy, and an instant later added in amazement: "Old Lacy and one of his men are with them!"

"Yes. And I bet that spells trouble for Jack and Fred," announced his brother.

The old farmer would not stop for the boys on the roadside, but drove directly to the Colby Hall entrance.

"Why! what's the matter?" exclaimed Randy to the military instructor.

"A little trouble, boys," was Captain Dale's answer. "You'll hear about it later." And then he went after the wagon, and the boys took to their heels and followed.

"Now then, you do what you promised!" snapped Elias Lacy, after Jack and Fred had jumped from the wagon. "Don't let 'em run away, nohow!"

"You can rest assured that I will take care of them, Mr. Lacy," answered the captain coldly.

"When do you expect Colonel Colby back?"

"Some time this afternoon."

"Then I guess I'll be back by that time to see him. An' I guess

I'll be able to prove them boys is guilty, too."

"Why, Jack! what is it all about?" demanded Randy, while his twin looked on questioningly. The boys' shotguns and game had been taken from the farm wagon, and now the pair from the Lacy farm drove away.

"You've got to search me!" declared Jack. "Old Lacy accuses Fred and me of shooting two of his cows."

"You didn't do it, though, did you?" queried Andy.

"Certainly not!" burst out Fred. "All we know about it is what he has told us. We weren't even near the pasture where the cows were kept."

As well as they were able, Jack and Fred explained the situation to their cousins and also answered a number of questions put to them by Captain Dale. The military instructor was much puzzled over the situation, and hardly knew what to do.

"You heard what I promised Mr. Lacy," he said finally. "I'll have to place you in the guardroom until Colonel Colby gets back. But I imagine you would rather be kept there than let Mr. Lacy take you down to the town lock-up."

"It isn't fair to lock us up at all," grumbled Fred. "We have done no wrong. Of course we stayed away from the Hall over night, but that couldn't be helped. It was no fun staying outdoors on such a cold night without shelter."

"Can't you parole us, Captain?" queried Jack.

"No. I gave Mr. Lacy my word that I would lock you up, and I'll have to do it. I'll see to it, however, that you suffer no discomforts while you are in the guardroom."

After this there seemed no help for it, and, turning their guns and game over to the twins, Jack and Fred followed Captain Dale through one of the lower corridors and then into a wing of the building. Here there was a room about twelve feet square, the one window of which was barred, and this was known officially as the school guardroom, or prison.

"You may wash up if you care to do so, and I will send you some breakfast," announced Captain Dale, and then left them in the room, locking the door behind him.

The apartment was but scantily furnished, containing an iron cot, a couple of stools, a table, and, in one corner, a wash bowl with running water. There was a small steam radiator in the room, and this the boys lost no time in turning on, for the air was damp and cold.

"This is a fine prospect, truly," remarked Fred, as he sank down on one of the stools. "I wonder how long we'll have to stay in this hole."

"That remains to be seen, Fred. I wish Colonel Colby were here. I think he would give us some good advice—being such an old friend of our fathers."

"Gee! I'd hate to have him send a letter home telling the folks that we were guilty of shooting a farmer's cows."

"So would I. I don't see how we are going to clear ourselves. You can bet Lacy will make out the blackest possible case against us."

After their outing in the woods the boys were glad enough to wash themselves. They had hardly finished when one of the waiters of the Hall came in with a large tray filled with an appetizing breakfast.

"This isn't so bad," declared Jack, when they had been left once more alone. The boys ate heartily, yet they were so much troubled that it is not likely the food did them any good.

The report soon circulated throughout Colby Hall that Jack and Fred had been placed under arrest, and many of the cadets wanted to know what it meant.

"They've been arrested for shooting two of old Lacy's cows!" said Codfish, who had heard the news and had started to circulate it as quickly as possible. "They say old Lacy is going to send them to state's prison for it."

"Spikeless mosquitoes!" cried Fatty. "Do you think they really went over there and shot the cows?"

"I don't know, I'm sure," answered Walt Baxter, who was present. "I know they didn't bear old Lacy much good-will. They felt rather raw over the way the old man held 'em up with his shotgun when they were having their Hallowe'en fun."

"Yes. And they were down on Lacy because he once took away some chestnuts they had gathered from one of his trees," put in another cadet.

"Shooting cows is rather a serious business," was Bart White's comment.

This talk took place on the campus. Down in the gymnasium another group of cadets had gathered, including Nappy Martell and Slugger Brown.

Arthur M. Winfield

"Locked up for killing old Lacy's cows, eh?" cried Martell, with a satisfied grin on his face. "They'll catch it for that, all right enough!"

"I don't see why Colonel Colby don't fire 'em out of the school for it," said Slugger Brown.

"Maybe he will dismiss 'em if he finds out the report is true," ventured another cadet.

"Of course the report is true!" put in Codfish, who had come up. "Didn't one of the hired men see 'em do it?"

"Is that so, Codfish?"

"So they say."

"Oh, it would be just like those Rovers to do something like that," came from Nappy Martell. "They are that kind of fellows."

"I always thought they were pretty good chaps," was the comment of another cadet.

"Good chaps!" sneered Slugger Brown. "That shows you don't know 'em as well as we do. They are sneaks—all of 'em—and wouldn't hesitate a minute to do anything under-handed. I hope Colonel Colby gets after them and fires 'em out;" and then, with a knowing look at Martell, Slugger passed on, and presently his crony followed him.

A good deal of this talk drifted to the ears of the Rover twins and hurt them not a little. But they were in no position to combat what was said.

"Of course we know Jack and Fred are innocent," remarked

Randy to his brother. "But in a court of law it is one thing to know it and quite another thing to prove it."

"Yet I've always heard it said that a man was innocent until he was proved guilty," asserted Andy.

"Very true. Just the same, many a man has been convicted on what they call circumstantial evidence; and evidently the circumstantial evidence against Jack and Fred is pretty strong."

In the guardroom the time for Jack and Fred passed slowly. They discussed the situation from every possible point of view, but without arriving at any satisfactory conclusion.

"Even if they don't send us to prison for the crime, they may make our fathers' pay for the cows," said Jack.

"Yes. And Colonel Colby may send us home," added Fred, dismally. "Oh, dear! wouldn't that be the worst ever?" and he sank down on the cot and covered his face with his hands.

It was Martell and Brown, aided by Codfish, who saw to it that the report of Jack and Fred's arrest was carried to Clearwater Hall. This brought consternation to the girls, particularly to Ruth and May.

"I won't believe it!" declared Ruth. "I don't believe Jack and Fred would be so mean."

"I don't believe it either!" cried Spouter's cousin. "Somebody else must have done it!"

In the middle of the afternoon Colonel Colby returned to the Hall and was at once acquainted with the affair by Captain Dale. The colonel was on the point of questioning the two prisoners when a servant came in, announcing the arrival of Elias Lacy. The farmer was as wildly excited as he had been in the morning.

"I knowed I was right!" he cried, flourishing a letter in the colonel's face. "Here's something I got to prove it! It come by mail this mornin' when I was bringin' them young whelps over here. I put the letter in my pocket, an' I forgot all about it until an hour ago. Jest read that, will you?" and he thrust the communication into Colonel Colby's hand.

The letter was postmarked at Beach Haven, and had been mailed the evening previous. It was written in a slanting backhand, evidently disguised, and ran as follows:

"Dear Mr. Lacy:

"Your two cows were shot by Jack Rover and Fred Rover. They were out in the woods hunting when we saw them go towards your pasture lot. We thought they were up to some trick, so watched them. They drove the two cows from the rest of the herd, and then Jack Rover gave one cow two shots and Fred Rover gave the other cow two shots. Then they ran back into the woods as tight as they could go. They didn't join the other hunters they had gone out with, most likely because they were afraid.

"You had better go to Colby Hall and have them arrested before they run away.

"Yours truly,

"Three boys who know, but who do not dare to give you their names."

CHAPTER XXIX

THE EXPOSURE

"There! what do you think of that letter?" demanded Elias Lacy, after Colonel Colby had read the communication.

"I don't know what to think of it, Mr. Lacy," was the slow reply. "I have not yet had an opportunity to interview the two Rovers. If you will sit down here in my office, I'll talk to them and try to settle this matter with you."

"Don't you want me to go with you?" questioned the old farmer quickly.

"No. I prefer to interview them alone."

"All right then, I'll stay here. But don't be too long, 'cause I want to drive down to the town an' git Bill Pixley, the chief o' police, or one of his men."

"I don't think you'll need any police, Mr. Lacy. I think we'll be able to fix this matter up to your entire satisfaction," answered Colonel Colby; and then left the office and made his way along the corridors to the guardroom.

His coming was a great relief to Jack and Fred, for they felt

Arthur M. Winfield

that in Colonel Colby they had a real friend. Yet they were much troubled, for they realized that the case looked black against them.

"Now tell me everything you know. Don't hold back a single item," said the colonel, as he seated himself on one of the stools.

Thereupon both cadets related their story in detail—how they had gone out with Frank Newberry and the others, how the two parties had become separated, and how they had lost their way, camped out over night, and finally found the woods road leading down to the Lacy farm, and then how Elias Lacy and his hired man had held them up and threatened them with arrest.

"And you do not know a single thing about the shooting of the cows?" questioned the colonel, eyeing them sternly.

"Not a thing, sir," responded Jack, promptly.

"We don't know anything more about those cows than you do, sir," added Fred, vehemently. "We weren't anywhere near his place when they were shot."

"Then what do you two say to this letter?" continued the master of Colby Hall, and presented the communication to them.

Jack read the letter with Fred looking over his shoulder. Then, of a sudden, Fred gave a cry of amazement.

"I think I know who wrote that letter!" he exclaimed.

"You do!" returned Colonel Colby and Jack, simultaneously.

"I think so; although, of course, I am not sure." Fred looked at his cousin. "It would be just like him to do it."

"Who are you talking about, Fred?"

"I'm talking about Slugger Brown."

"Slugger Brown!"

"Do you mean Slogwell Brown?" queried the master of the school.

"Yes, sir."

"And what makes you think Brown wrote that communication?" demanded Colonel Colby. And now, somewhat to their wonder, the Rovers realized that the colonel seemed to be unusually interested.

"Because I once saw Brown writing in backhand fashion on the blackboard in the gymnasium," explained Fred. "He wrote a hand almost identical with that. I noticed it particularly, because he was amusing himself by writing one line slanting backward and the next line slanting forward."

"Did he know you were watching him?"

"Oh, no! I didn't stay there long enough for that. He was all alone, and as I didn't care to speak to him, I passed out without his noticing it."

"How long ago was this?"

"Only about a week ago."

"Hum!" The colonel mused for a moment, knitting his brows

closely as he did so. "That is worth investigating." He thought for another moment. "You have nothing more to add to your story?"

"No, sir," answered Fred.

"I think we've told you everything, Colonel Colby," returned Jack. "We are innocent, and I trust you will do all you can to help us prove it."

"I shall do what is absolutely fair in the matter," answered Colonel Colby; and then left the two boys once more to themselves.

Andy and Randy had begged for permission to talk things over with their cousins, and they came in to see Jack and Fred almost immediately after Colonel Colby left.

"If Slugger Brown wrote that letter, maybe he and Nappy Martell did the shooting," remarked Randy.

"They would be just mean enough to do it," added his twin. "They'd do anything to get our crowd into trouble."

"Why can't you two fellows watch Brown and Martell?" questioned Jack. "You might tell Gif and Spouter and Ned about it, too. Find out where those two fellows were yesterday afternoon, and find out if they used any of the shotguns."

"Say! that's an idea!" cried Randy, enthusiastically. "I'll go at it right away!"

"And so will I!" declared his brother. "Maybe we'll be able to lay the whole blame on that pair."

The twins talked it over with the others for a little while longer, and then were let out of the guardroom by a servant, who locked the door after them. As they came out into the main corridor of the Hall, they saw that Elias Lacy was just leaving Colonel Colby's office.

"All right, then, I'll wait," the old farmer was saying. "But I'll be back by to-morrow afternoon, an' if you can't prove by that time that them Rover boys is innercent, I'm a-goin' to have 'em locked up."

"Very well, Mr. Lacy," the colonel replied, and bowed his visitor out of the door.

"Well, anyway, the colonel has got old Lacy to wait another day," whispered Randy. "That will give us just so much more time to get on the track of what Martell and Brown have been doing."

"All provided they are really guilty of playing this dirty trick," answered his brother.

In the upper hallway the twins ran across Ned Lowe, and immediately took that cadet into their confidence, and asked him if he would not try to find out for them where Brown and Martell had been the previous afternoon.

"For, you see, we can't ask them ourselves," explained Randy. "If we did that they would become suspicious at once."

"All right, I'll do what I can," answered Ned, and made off without delay. He came back in less than fifteen minutes, looking much excited.

"How did you make out?" queried Randy, eagerly.

"Great! I want you two fellows to come upstairs at once while Brown and Martell are out of their rooms. And I think you had better bring along one of the teachers as a witness."

"Why, what have you learned, Ned?" questioned Andy.

"I saw them down near the gymnasium, and sneaked up behind them, and by rare good luck heard them talking about two shotguns that belonged in the gun rack. They were wondering how they could get them from their rooms back into the gun rack without detection."

"Hurrah! I wager we have found 'em out!" ejaculated Randy, excitedly. "Come on! let's get one of the teachers at once!"

The boys were fortunate enough to fall in with Professor Brice a minute later, and in a rather excited fashion they told the teacher of what they had learned and what they proposed to do.

"Why, certainly, I'll go with you," said Paul Brice, quickly. "I want just as much as anybody to get at the bottom of this affair."

Accompanied by the professor, the three cadets hurried to the second floor of the Hall and then to the rooms occupied by Slugger Brown and Nappy Martell. The door to each was locked, but one of them was opened for the crowd by an assistant janitor. A hasty search revealed nothing in the shape of a firearm in either room, and the Rover boys were much disappointed. But then Randy thought of the bed, and quickly raised the mattress. On the springs rested a shotgun.

"And I'll bet the other shotgun is in the other bed!" cried Andy, and he and the professor made an investigation. The fun-loving Rover's surmise was correct.

"These are guns belonging to the Hall, too!" cried Ned, pointing out the mark of the school on the stocks. "They must belong down in the gun rack, just as Slugger and Martell said."

"Bring those guns along, boys, and we'll go directly to Colonel Colby's office," said Professor Brice; and the cadets lost no time in doing as he directed.

They found the master of the school seated at his desk, looking over a mass of papers. He gazed in wonder at the three lads and Professor Brice.

"We found the shotguns that were used on those cows!" cried Randy, his eyes sparkling.

"And do you know where we found 'em? In the beds that Slugger Brown and Nappy Martell use!" broke in Andy.

"What's this?" And now the colonel was really startled.

"You had better let the boys tell the beginning of the story, and I will tell the end," said Professor Brice.

Thereupon, the two Rovers repeated the talk that had taken place in the guardroom, and then told how they had gotten Ned to spy on Brown and Martell. Then Ned told of what he had heard, and of how the three had called on Professor Brice for assistance. After that the teacher took up the narrative, ending with the finding of the shotguns in the beds.

"It looks like a pretty clear case against Brown and Martell," remarked the colonel slowly. "However, I shall have to make a further investigation. I will send for Brown and Martell at once."

Arthur M. Winfield

The colonel was as good as his word, and inside of five minutes Slugger and Nappy came into the office together. They looked much disturbed, and this look increased when they saw Andy and Randy.

"Brown and Martell, I have sent for you to answer a few questions," began Colonel Colby, sternly, as the two cadets faced him. "I want you to answer me directly and truthfully. What was your object in taking two of our shotguns from the gun rack and going over to Mr. Lacy's farm and shooting down two of his cows?"

"Wh—wh—why, wh—wh—what do you mean?" faltered Brown.

"We didn't—er—shoot—er—any cows," stammered Martell.

Both boys were thrown into utter confusion, and showed it plainly. Then Slugger Brown suddenly turned to glare at the Rovers.

"Is this some of your work?" he demanded. "If it is, let me tell you I'll pay you back for it!"

"Stop that talk, Brown!" commanded Colonel Colby. "I want you and Martell to answer my question. Why did you go over there and shoot those cows?"

"Who says we shot the cows?" questioned Nappy, faintly.

"Never mind who says so. You did it, and it is useless for you to deny it. Here are the two guns you took from the gun rack and afterwards hid in your beds. And here is the despicable note you, Brown, wrote and mailed to Mr. Lacy," and the colonel held out the communication.

"Oh, Colonel Colby, I di—di—didn't do it!" faltered Slugger Brown. His face had suddenly gone white, and he could scarcely speak.

"Do you deny that this is your handwriting?"

"I—I—Oh, is—I—I—didn't—That is—" and here Slugger Brown broke down absolutely, not knowing what to say.

"Did you mail that letter or did Brown do it?" questioned the colonel, quickly turning to Martell.

"He did it! I didn't have anything to do with it!" burst out Nappy, breaking down completely.

"It ain't so!" cried Slugger. "He was with me, and he dropped the letter in the post-office!"

"And so you killed the cows to get the Rovers into trouble?" said Colonel Colby; and now his eyes glittered like steel. "A fine thing to do, truly! I did not think any of our cadets would stoop to such a base action."

"It was a—er—a joke," gasped Nappy.

"A joke! To kill two valuable cows? Martell, if you talk that way, I'll be inclined to think you are losing your senses. But evidently there is something radically wrong with both you and Brown," went on the master of the Hall. "This case of the cows and the plot against the Rovers is bad enough, but I have another matter against you which may prove even worse."

"What is that?" questioned Slugger, very faintly.

"It is a case that Captain Larkins of the steam tug, *Mary D.*, has lodged against you. He says he has absolute proof that both of you went out in a motor boat one day and tampered with the towing line and the chains of a large lumber raft, so that when a sudden squall came up on the lake, the towing line parted and the lumber raft went to pieces."

"Oh, say! that must have been the squall we were out in!" exclaimed Randy. "And we got caught among that floating lumber, too!"

"Yes, that was the time," answered Colonel Colby.

"Oh, Colonel! can't we go to our cousins and tell them that they can have their freedom?" questioned Andy, with a sudden thought of those left in the guardroom.

"Yes, Rover. Both of you and also Lowe can go," was the colonel's reply. "I will settle this affair with Brown and Martell."

"And will you settle it with Mr. Lacy, too?" queried Randy, quickly.

"Yes. I will fix the whole matter up. You may tell Jack and Fred that they need not worry any further on this score." And thereupon Andy, Randy and Ned hurried away to bear the glad tidings to the prisoners.

Of course Jack and Fred were greatly pleased to be released. They listened eagerly to all the twins and Ned had to relate.

"So Nappy and Slugger are guilty!" cried Jack. "What a mean way to act!"

"And to think they are also guilty of sending that lumber adrift," said Fred. "They'll suffer for that."

"They ought to suffer," answered his cousin.

CHAPTER XXX

A FOOTBALL VICTORY—CONCLUSION

"Whoop her up for Colby Hall!"

"This is the time Columbus Academy wins!"

"Not on your life! This is Colby Hall day!"

"You'll sing a different tune after the game is over!"

"Hurrah! here come the elevens now!"

And then a wild shouting, intermingled with the tooting of horns and the sounding of rattles, rent the air, while banners went waving on every side.

It was the day of the great game between Colby Hall and Columbus Academy. It had been decided that the contest should take place on the field belonging to the military academy, and once again everything had been put in the best of order for this gala occasion. The grandstand and the bleachers were overflowing with spectators, and in a distant field were parked a hundred automobiles or more, while in another field were numerous carriages and farm wagons.

Arthur M. Winfield

"We've certainly got a crowd to-day," remarked Randy, who, with his brother, was in the section of the stand reserved for the Colbyites and their friends. In front of the twins and their chums sat Ruth, May, and half a dozen other girls from Clearwater Hall.

"I don't see anything of Nappy Martell or Slugger Brown," remarked Ida Brierley, who was with the girls.

"I hope you don't want to see them, Ida," returned Ruth, promptly.

"Indeed, I do not!" answered the other girl. "I was only wondering what had become of them."

"Jack told me they had both left the Hall for the term. They shot those cows, you know, and they had some other trouble which was hushed up."

"Oh, that was the trouble over that lumber raft," put in Jennie Mason.

"Right you are!" answered Andy, bending over and speaking in a low tone so that no outsider might hear. "Their folks had to pony up a pretty penny, too, for the lumber and for the cows."

"Oh, well, let's forget Martell and Brown," broke in May. "I want to enjoy this game."

"And that's what we all want to do," said Alice Strobell.

What had been said concerning Slugger Brown and Nappy Martell was true. Questioned by Colonel Colby, the two misguided cadets had finally broken down utterly and confessed everything, telling how they had once gotten into a quarrel with Captain Larkins on the lake and how they had sought to get square by tampering with the fastenings of the lumber raft and the towline; and they had also related the particulars of how they had watched Jack and Fred go out shooting and had then purloined the two shotguns from the gun rack and hurried over to the Lacy farm to shoot the cows. Mr. Brown and Mr. Martell had been called upon to pay both the lake captain and the old farmer heavy damages; and thereupon they had withdrawn their sons from the Hall for the time being.

"And I'm glad they're gone," had been Fred's comment. "I hope they never come back here again."

"Yes, we could do without Brown and Martell very well," had been Jack's answer.

Both of the cousins were particularly happy on this day. Jack occupied his former position on the eleven, and Fred had been drafted from the scrub team and put on the substitutes' bench in place of Brown.

"Maybe I'll get a chance to play!" cried the youngest Rover eagerly, when the football captain brought him the news.

"Perhaps so, Fred," answered Gif. "Although, of course, I hope none of our players get hurt."

As the Colby Hall eleven marched out on the gridiron, Jack glanced towards the grandstand and caught Ruth's eye. The girl gaily waved a Colby Hall banner at him. Then May caught sight of Fred on the side lines, and shook her hand at him.

Spectators from the town were almost as much interested in the contest as were the two schools. This football game was

Arthur M. Winfield

always the big match of the season, and many wagers were placed on the result. In the past the contests had always been exceedingly bitter, with the various scores almost a tie, Columbus Academy winning by a narrow margin one year and Colby Hall taking the lead by an equally narrow margin the following year.

When the Columbus Academy boys came out on the field, it was seen that they were good, husky fellows, every bit as heavy as the Colby Hall eleven. They looked in the pink of condition.

"I am afraid our boys will have their work cut out for them in this game," remarked Mr. Crews to Colonel Colby.

"Well, our boys look pretty fit," answered the master of the Hall.

By the toss of a coin, Columbus Academy won the choice of position, and took the west goal, the slight wind that was blowing being in their favor. Then the two teams lined up for the kick-off.

"Now then, boys, show 'em what you can do!" yelled the Colby Hall cadets, and then the school slogan rang out on the air.

"Put it all over 'em, boys!" yelled one of the Columbus Academy followers. "Come on now, all together!" he added, and started up a song, the refrain of which contained the line: "We're here to-day to bury them!"

"What an awful song to sing!" remarked Ruth.

"Oh, you mustn't mind that," returned Andy, gaily. "He sings best who sings last, as the cat said to the bird."

It must be confessed that both teams were rather nervous at the outset of the contest. The play was decidedly ragged, and one or two mistakes were made, which, however, profited neither side anything. The ball was carried first to the Colby Hall 10-yard line, and from there it went back to the Columbus 15-yard line, and then it sawed back and forth until eight minutes of the first quarter had passed.

"Gee! this begins to look like a blank," was Spouter's comment.

"So it does," returned Dan Soppinger. "Say! can any of you tell me why the—"

"Don't ask questions now, Dan," interrupted Randy. "Oh, look! look!" he burst out suddenly. "Isn't that great!"

The ball had dribbled back and forth until, by a punt, it reached Colby Hall's 20-yard line. It landed close to Jack, and like a flash he gathered it to his breast and started for the Columbus goal.

"Go it, Rover! go it!"

"Don't let 'em down you, Jack!"

With his friends cheering lustily, Jack sped on, dodging many straight-arm tackles, and skipping from right to left and then back again in order to avoid the numerous players who seemed to confront him as if by magic. Then somebody appeared on his left, and the next moment he went down with a thud, not knowing where he had landed.

"It's a touchdown!" was the cry, and then the Colby Hall followers went wild with delight, while Columbus Academy was mute. The girls stood up in the grandstand and waved their banners gaily.

"Oh, just to think, Jack did it!" murmured Ruth, and her face showed her intense satisfaction.

"Now if only Walt Baxter can kick a goal!" cried Randy.

But this was not to be, for at the moment the leather sailed through the air, a strong puff of wind came up and the ball went just outside the posts.

"Well, never mind," cried Randy, consolingly; "that puts us in the lead."

The run had somewhat exhausted Jack, but still he insisted upon keeping on playing, and after the wonderful exhibition he had made, Gif had not the heart to call in a substitute to take his place.

But if, with a touchdown in their favor, Colby thought to remain in the lead, they soon had this hope shattered. The Columbus Academy eleven played a fast and snappy second quarter, and, as a result, before it was half over they took the ball on a fumble and circled the left end for twelve yards.

"Say, that's going some," remarked Fatty.

"Oh, it won't net them anything," responded Andy.

But in this he was wrong, for on the next two plays Columbus carried the ball over the line for a touchdown.

"A tie! A tie!" yelled the followers of the Academy.

"Now then, boys, don't miss the goal!"

"It isn't likely they'll miss it," grumbled Andy. "The wind is in their favor." The goal was kicked with ease, and then the score stood: Columbus Academy—7, Colby Hall—6.

During the intermission between the second and third quarters, Gif and Mr. Crews gave the eleven some very pointed instructions. One player had hurt his ankle slightly, and he was taken out and a substitute took his place. But the substitute was not Fred, much to that youth's disappointment.

If the first and second quarters had been fast and snappy, the third quarter was even more so. Back and forth went the ball, and it was lost both by Colby Hall and by the Academy team. There were some really fine tackles and splendid runs, but all of these availed nothing. And when the whistle blew the score still stood 6 for Colby Hall as against 7 for Columbus Academy.

"Tough luck!" groaned Ned.

"Oh, we're going to win—I'm sure of it!" answered Randy.

"I hope what you say proves true," returned Ruth, hopefully.

Just before the whistle was given for the end of the third quarter there had been a grand crash and a fierce mix-up on the field. Then it was found that both a Columbus Academy player and a Colby Hall youth would have to be taken out of the game.

"Now then, Fred, here's your chance," said Gif, coming up to the youngest Rover. "I'm going to put you in, and I want you to help us win the game."

"Win it is!" cried Fred, his eyes shining eagerly. "We'll either win or we'll die!"

Arthur M. Winfield

When the whistle blew for the final quarter, all of the players who trooped on the field had a do-or-die expression on their faces. Once more the play became fast and furious, and, as a result, in less than three minutes Columbus Academy scored another touchdown, which, however, failed of a goal.

"Hurrah! That's the way to do it!" yelled their followers in keen delight.

"Brace up, boys! brace up! This won't do at all. Come on now, all together!" And then Colby Hall went in with renewed vigor so that inside of a few minutes more they, too, had scored another touchdown, and from this they managed to kick a goal.

"Hello! what do you know about that! Another tie!"

"Thirteen to thirteen! Same as that other game! Say, this is getting mighty interesting!"

So far, Fred, although he had played as hard as anybody in the game, had failed to make any appreciable showing. Now, however, with only a few minutes to spare, he saw his chance.

One of the Columbus Academy players had dropped back for a punt. Fred, who was close at hand, made a sudden leap over a protecting half back and blocked the kick.

"Say, look at that! Fred Rover is in the game for keeps!"

"Send it back, Fred! Send it back!"

The words were scarcely spoken when the thrilled spectators saw that the youngest Rover boy had the leather. Like a flash he sent it rolling back, Gif coming to his aid.

"A safety! A safety for Colby Hall!"

"Hurrah! that puts Colby two points ahead!"

"Good work for Fred Rover!"

"Now then, Colby Hall, you've got 'em a-going! Keep it up!"

"Pitch into 'em, Columbus! Pitch into 'em!"

So the yelling went on while all of the spectators stood up in their seats, anxious to see what might be accomplished next. But there was no time to do more. The whistle blew and the great game was over.

Colby Hall had won!

In a twinkling the huge field was covered with spectators running in all directions, and the victorious eleven was surrounded. Many were the congratulations showered on all the players, and it may well be believed that Jack and Fred came in for their full share.

"The finest game I ever saw," declared Colonel Colby, as he shook hands with all his youthful players.

"Oh, Jack! It was simply grand—that run you made!" exclaimed Ruth, when she saw him.

"Yes. And the way you played for that safety!" put in May to Fred.

Columbus Academy was much disheartened over its defeat, yet it cheered the victors and was cheered in return; and then the great crowd gradually dispersed.

"Bonfire to-night, boys! And a big one, too!" cried Andy, as he rushed up to fairly embrace both his cousins. Then, to work off some of his high spirits, the acrobatic youth turned several cartwheels and handsprings.

"What a pity our folks weren't here to see this game," said Jack, wistfully.

"Never mind, we'll write them all the particulars," announced Randy. "And we'll send them copies of the local paper, too. That will have a full account of it," and this was done as soon as possible.

After the game refreshments were served to the cadets and their particular friends, and in this, of course, the Rovers and the girls from Clearwater Hall joined. Then the boys took the girls back to their school in an automobile.

"We are certainly having one dandy time at this school," remarked Fred, on the way back to Colby Hall.

"Right you are!" answered Randy.

"If only we hadn't had that trouble with Slugger and Nappy," remarked Jack.

"Oh, don't bother about those fellows!" cried Andy. "I don't believe they'll ever trouble any of us again."

But in this he was mistaken. Brown and Martell did trouble them, and in what manner will be related in the next volume of this series, to be entitled: "The Rover Boys on Snowshoe Island; or, The Old Lumberman's Treasure Box."

In that volume we shall meet all the boys and their chums again, and also learn the particulars of a queer mystery, and also of a great joke played upon Professor Asa Lemm.

The cadets of Colby Hall were a happy crowd that night. A great bonfire blazed along the bank of the river, and around this the boys cut up to their hearts' content. Then they marched around and around the Hall, singing loudly.

"It's certainly a dandy school, isn't it?" remarked Jack to his cousins.

"The best ever!" they answered in a chorus. And here for the present we will leave the Rover boys and say good-bye.

THE END

Arthur M. Winfield

Choose from Thousands of 1stWorldLibrary Classics By

A. M. Barnard
Ada Leverson
Adolphus William Ward
Aesop
Agatha Christie
Alexander Aaronsohn
Alexander Kielland
Alexandre Dumas
Alfred Gatty
Alfred Ollivant
Alice Duer Miller
Alice Turner Curtis
Alice Dunbar
Allen Chapman
Alleyne Ireland
Ambrose Bierce
Amelia E. Barr
Amory H. Bradford
Andrew Lang
Andrew McFarland Davis
Andy Adams
Angela Brazil
Anna Alice Chapin
Anna Sewell
Annie Besant
Annie Hamilton Donnell
Annie Payson Call
Annie Roe Carr
Annonaymous
Anton Chekhov
Archibald Lee Fletcher
Arnold Bennett
Arthur C. Benson
Arthur Conan Doyle
Arthur M. Winfield
Arthur Ransome
Arthur Schnitzler
Arthur Train
Atticus
B.H. Baden-Powell
B. M. Bower
B. C. Chatterjee
Baroness Emmuska Orczy
Baroness Orczy
Basil King
Bayard Taylor
Ben Macomber
Bertha Muzzy Bower
Bjornstjerne Bjornson

Booth Tarkington
Boyd Cable
Bram Stoker
C. Collodi
C. E. Orr
C. M. Ingleby
Carolyn Wells
Catherine Parr Traill
Charles A. Eastman
Charles Amory Beach
Charles Dickens
Charles Dudley Warner
Charles Farrar Browne
Charles Ives
Charles Kingsley
Charles Klein
Charles Hanson Towne
Charles Lathrop Pack
Charles Romyn Dake
Charles Whibley
Charles Willing Beale
Charlotte M. Braeme
Charlotte M. Yonge
Charlotte Perkins Stetson
Clair W. Hayes
Clarence Day Jr.
Clarence E. Mulford
Clemence Housman
Confucius
Coningsby Dawson
Cornelis DeWitt Wilcox
Cyril Burleigh
D. H. Lawrence
Daniel Defoe
David Garnett
Dinah Craik
Don Carlos Janes
Donald Keyhoe
Dorothy Kilner
Dougan Clark
Douglas Fairbanks
E. Nesbit
E. P. Roe
E. Phillips Oppenheim
E. S. Brooks
Earl Barnes
Edgar Rice Burroughs
Edith Van Dyne
Edith Wharton

Edward Everett Hale
Edward J. O'Biren
Edward S. Ellis
Edwin L. Arnold
Eleanor Atkins
Eleanor Hallowell Abbott
Eliot Gregory
Elizabeth Gaskell
Elizabeth McCracken
Elizabeth Von Arnim
Ellem Key
Emerson Hough
Emilie F. Carlen
Emily Bronte
Emily Dickinson
Enid Bagnold
Enilor Macartney Lane
Erasmus W. Jones
Ernie Howard Pie
Ethel May Dell
Ethel Turner
Ethel Watts Mumford
Eugene Sue
Eugenie Foa
Eugene Wood
Eustace Hale Ball
Evelyn Everett-green
Everard Cotes
F. H. Cheley
F. J. Cross
F. Marion Crawford
Fannie E. Newberry
Federick Austin Ogg
Ferdinand Ossendowski
Fergus Hume
Florence A. Kilpatrick
Fremont B. Deering
Francis Bacon
Francis Darwin
Frances Hodgson Burnett
Frances Parkinson Keyes
Frank Gee Patchin
Frank Harris
Frank Jewett Mather
Frank L. Packard
Frank V. Webster
Frederic Stewart Isham
Frederick Trevor Hill
Frederick Winslow Taylor

Friedrich Kerst	Hayden Carruth	James Branch Cabell
Friedrich Nietzsche	Helent Hunt Jackson	James DeMille
Fyodor Dostoyevsky	Helen Nicolay	James Joyce
G.A. Henty	Hendrik Conscience	James Lane Allen
G.K. Chesterton	Hendy David Thoreau	James Lane Allen
Gabrielle E. Jackson	Henri Barbusse	James Oliver Curwood
Garrett P. Serviss	Henrik Ibsen	James Oppenheim
Gaston Leroux	Henry Adams	James Otis
George A. Warren	Henry Ford	James R. Driscoll
George Ade	Henry Frost	Jane Abbott
Geroge Bernard Shaw	Henry James	Jane Austen
George Cary Eggleston	Henry Jones Ford	Jane L. Stewart
George Durston	Henry Seton Merriman	Janet Aldridge
George Ebers	Henry W Longfellow	Jens Peter Jacobsen
George Eliot	Herbert A. Giles	Jerome K. Jerome
George Gissing	Herbert Carter	Jessie Graham Flower
George MacDonald	Herbert N. Casson	John Buchan
George Meredith	Herman Hesse	John Burroughs
George Orwell	Hildegard G. Frey	John Cournos
George Sylvester Viereck	Homer	John F. Kennedy
George Tucker	Honore De Balzac	John Gay
George W. Cable	Horace B. Day	John Glasworthy
George Wharton James	Horace Walpole	John Habberton
Gertrude Atherton	Horatio Alger Jr.	John Joy Bell
Gordon Casserly	Howard Pyle	John Kendrick Bangs
Grace E. King	Howard R. Garis	John Milton
Grace Gallatin	Hugh Lofting	John Philip Sousa
Grace Greenwood	Hugh Walpole	John Taintor Foote
Grant Allen	Humphry Ward	Jonas Lauritz Idemil Lie
Guillermo A. Sherwell	Ian Maclaren	Jonathan Swift
Gulielma Zollinger	Inez Haynes Gillmore	Joseph A. Altsheler
Gustav Flaubert	Irving Bacheller	Joseph Carey
H. A. Cody	Isabel Cecilia Williams	Joseph Conrad
H. B. Irving	Isabel Hornibrook	Joseph E. Badger Jr
H.C. Bailey	Israel Abrahams	Joseph Hergesheimer
H. G. Wells	Ivan Turgenev	Joseph Jacobs
H. H. Munro	J.G.Austin	Jules Vernes
H. Irving Hancock	J. Henri Fabre	Julian Hawthrone
H. R. Naylor	J. M. Barrie	Julie A Lippmann
H. Rider Haggard	J. M. Walsh	Justin Huntly McCarthy
H. W. C. Davis	J. Macdonald Oxley	Kakuzo Okakura
Haldeman Julius	J. R. Miller	Karle Wilson Baker
Hall Caine	J. S. Fletcher	Kate Chopin
Hamilton Wright Mabie	J. S. Knowles	Kenneth Grahame
Hans Christian Andersen	J. Storer Clouston	Kenneth McGaffey
Harold Avery	J. W. Duffield	Kate Langley Bosher
Harold McGrath	Jack London	Kate Langley Bosher
Harriet Beecher Stowe	Jacob Abbott	Katherine Cecil Thurston
Harry Castlemon	James Allen	Katherine Stokes
Harry Coghill	James Andrews	L. A. Abbot
Harry Houidini	James Baldwin	L. T. Meade

L. Frank Baum
Latta Griswold
Laura Dent Crane
Laura Lee Hope
Laurence Housman
Lawrence Beasley
Leo Tolstoy
Leonid Andreyev
Lewis Carroll
Lewis Sperry Chafer
Lilian Bell
Lloyd Osbourne
Louis Hughes
Louis Joseph Vance
Louis Tracy
Louisa May Alcott
Lucy Fitch Perkins
Lucy Maud Montgomery
Luther Benson
Lydia Miller Middleton
Lyndon Orr
M. Corvus
M. H. Adams
Margaret E. Sangster
Margret Howth
Margaret Vandercook
Margaret W. Hungerford
Margret Penrose
Maria Edgeworth
Maria Thompson Daviess
Mariano Azuela
Marion Polk Angellotti
Mark Overton
Mark Twain
Mary Austin
Mary Catherine Crowley
Mary Cole
Mary Hastings Bradley
Mary Roberts Rinehart
Mary Rowlandson
M. Wollstonecraft Shelley
Maud Lindsay
Max Beerbohm
Myra Kelly
Nathaniel Hawthrone
Nicolo Machiavelli
O. F. Walton
Oscar Wilde

Owen Johnson
P.G. Wodehouse
Paul and Mabel Thorne
Paul G. Tomlinson
Paul Severing
Percy Brebner
Percy Keese Fitzhugh
Peter B. Kyne
Plato
Quincy Allen
R. Derby Holmes
R. L. Stevenson
R. S. Ball
Rabindranath Tagore
Rahul Alvares
Ralph Bonehill
Ralph Henry Barbour
Ralph Victor
Ralph Waldo Emmerson
Rene Descartes
Ray Cummings
Rex Beach
Rex E. Beach
Richard Harding Davis
Richard Jefferies
Richard Le Gallienne
Robert Barr
Robert Frost
Robert Gordon Anderson
Robert L. Drake
Robert Lansing
Robert Lynd
Robert Michael Ballantyne
Robert W. Chambers
Rosa Nouchette Carey
Rudyard Kipling
Saint Augustine
Samuel B. Allison
Samuel Hopkins Adams
Sarah Bernhardt
Sarah C. Hallowell
Selma Lagerlof
Sherwood Anderson
Sigmund Freud
Standish O'Grady
Stanley Weyman
Stella Benson
Stella M. Francis

Stephen Crane
Stewart Edward White
Stijn Streuvels
Swami Abhedananda
Swami Parmananda
T. S. Ackland
T. S. Arthur
The Princess Der Ling
Thomas A. Janvier
Thomas A Kempis
Thomas Anderton
Thomas Bailey Aldrich
Thomas Bulfinch
Thomas De Quincey
Thomas Dixon
Thomas H. Huxley
Thomas Hardy
Thomas More
Thornton W. Burgess
U. S. Grant
Upton Sinclair
Valentine Williams
Various Authors
Vaughan Kester
Victor Appleton
Victor G. Durham
Victoria Cross
Virginia Woolf
Wadsworth Camp
Walter Camp
Walter Scott
Washington Irving
Wilbur Lawton
Wilkie Collins
Willa Cather
Willard F. Baker
William Dean Howells
William le Queux
W. Makepeace Thackeray
William W. Walter
William Shakespeare
Winston Churchill
Yei Theodora Ozaki
Yogi Ramacharaka
Young E. Allison
Zane Grey